OVERCOMING NEGATIVE EMOTIONS

\

OVERCOMING
NEGATIVE
EMOTIONS

Marilee Donivan

SMB
Sunrise Mountain Books
Boise, Idaho

OVERCOMING NEGATIVE EMOTIONS
Copyright ©2017 Marilee Donivan

Front cover image ©ximagination; Chapter 6 photo ©Amnuai Batala; Pressure cooker graphic: Peter C. Espina; Back cover image ©dolgachov

ISBN 978-1-940728-04-9

Library of Congress Control Number: 2017904840

Published by Sunrise Mountain Books
13347 W. Tapatio Drive
Boise, Idaho 83713
www.sunrisemountainbooks.com

Printed in the United States of America

CONTENTS

1 What is Rattling my Sense of Well-being ?

Anxiety disorders, panic attacks, feelings of fear, uncertainty, regrets, depression, and inadequacy are increasingly afflicting men, women, teens, and children in recent years. People are feeling helpless and hopeless. Medical and social researchers are recording growing numbers of trips to emergency rooms by patients who have symptoms of heart attacks, subsequently diagnosed as anxiety and panic attacks rather than from underlying cardiac diseases.

What's going on?

Television, movies, social media, busyness, lack of down time, lack of contemplation time, lack of play time, and lack of relaxation time are all contributing to a wild sense of "The world is not a safe place," "There just isn't enough time to get everything done," "Life is too hard," "I'm not good enough," "I'm not successful," "Terrible things happen every day," "Will I be safe when I leave my house?"

We are bombarded with terrible news every day. Sights and sounds of war, danger, shootings, shouts, deceitful actions, medical warnings, exposés of persons in authority whom we thought we could trust, unexpected and unprovoked attacks, vicious language, horror, and assaults of all kinds. Even while watching a sporting event or benign entertainment, we must endure ugly movie trailers that jar our senses. With our minds filled with such a preponderance of images and impressions, it is no wonder that the images persist even after we close our eyes and plug our ears.

At the other end of the spectrum, we hear from positive thinking gurus, "You can be anything you want," "You can do anything you want," "Just believe in yourself," "You, too, can be a millionaire." For most of us, that just isn't true. A statement like "The sky is the limit" stimulates the imagination, and raises expectations, but it disregards real differences between any two persons and their abilities, talents, and opportunities. When we hit the wall, encounter obstacles, or are aced out by a more talented competitor, we become disillusioned by our shattered dreams.

There are things in our lives that we cannot control, but there are also things in our lives that we have control over. The life skill we need is not how to dream largely enough. It is how to take stock of who we are, what we have to work with, our abilities, our interests, our inspiration, our talents, our resources, our opportunities, and our faith. Then we can move forward with a realistic vision of what we can do, what we can learn, and what we are willing to sacrifice to achieve that which we are created for.

Good premise. It works. But, why is it so hard to make this happen?

We have an enemy. Actually, make that plural. We have enemies who relentlessly work to disrupt our good intentions and desires. Our enemies are those negative emotions that interfere with a reasoned approach and reaction to people and events in our daily lives.

We all have people and events that have contributed to specific and general negative thoughts and emotions. But they do not have to have dominion over us all the time or all our lives. God has given us the breakthrough reality of His love, power, and instruction to overcome negative emotions no matter where we are in our lifespan. He is interested in our well-being. He meets us where we are to give us the peace of mind and joyful living that He intends for us to have.

Negative thinking can become a treacherous habit, but it is a habit that can be broken. When we are willing to be rid of negative emotions that hold us captive, there are steps that will help. Benjamin Disraeli said, "Nurture your mind with great thoughts, for you will never go higher than you THINK." He was right. Right thoughts lift us up, and free our minds to think creatively and live with anticipation of good things. Wrong thoughts pull us down and depress our energy and creativity, causing us to live with resignation, with our best hope being just to "make it through the day." The apostle Paul wrote to the Ephesians and reminded them to "be renewed in the spirit of your mind." The spirit of the mind is the way we think—our attitudes. When we renew the way we are thinking about things, our life changes along with it.

This is not a book of behavioral therapy although an aspect of it, specifically practice, is incorporated. This primarily is a book about the help God gives to release a new joyful freedom in the place of our emotional obstacles.

With God's help, great things can be accomplished beyond what even the best secular therapy can achieve. Therefore, many references will be given to encourage your faith and your confidence that God is working in you and for you as you turn your attitudes over to Him for renewal and transformation.

We will explore God's prescriptions to free us from debilitating feelings of fears and anxieties, false guilt, depression, lack of significance, inadequacy, body image, hopelessness, weakness, condemnation, and others.

We come from different life experiences and influences, looking for relief. Some of us are breathless, wondering if we even have time to sit down with a book like this. Some are feeling pressured, having been asked to squeeze in yet one more thing in the midst of a very busy and demanding schedule. We think we have our days carefully planned, but then an unexpected interruption comes just as we are ready to walk out the door. We long to be able to sit down and take a deep breath after what we hope was the last of our duties in an office, classroom, or home setting. We hope we will remember where we left off when it's time to resume the task.

I don't know about you, but one of my challenges is "out of sight, out of mind." My family knows how true this is of me. I will forget or get distracted if my unfinished work isn't right in front of me. Therefore, I have piles of papers on my desk, for fear that I will not know where I left off and where to begin the next day. It has to be in front of me when I sit down or it will be "layered" under other pressing things that holler for my attention. I lose Christmas presents that I buy early on sale, because I cannot remember where I put them for safe keeping. My family laughs each year when a Christmas present is delivered in March or July.

With encouragement, urgings, and suggestions from those who love me, I have tried all my life to get my Great Organization Challenge under control, but it doesn't budge. Systematic organization is a thinking style that is resident in one's way of processing information. Some people are more blessed with "organizational genes" than others. My daughter is one. She must have inherited it from her father. I was at the end of the line when those genes were handed out.

However, the emotional challenges I have needed to bring under control *have* been able to be changed! The principles I am sharing with you in this book really work. They work because emotions are at the center of how we relate to others, and God is all about relationships. The power of God's will for us and His work inside us through His Holy Spirit is designed for developing healthy relationships. It is perfect. We only need to desire it and cooperate with His will for our lives. It is a conscious decision. Not a passive one. We need to actively cooperate with God's plan for us as much as we can. It is how we receive the abundant life that Jesus said He came to give you and me.

We awaken each morning with a changing variety of emotions—anticipation, anxiety, desperation, excitement, uncertainty, weariness. All of us are ready for refreshment. We need it every day. Our great and wonderful God knows each of our needs intimately. Best of all, He cares and has planned this time for you to take a deep breath, to relax and be encouraged. Ready? Breathe!

*Please note:

Before launching into these principles and steps, it's important to note here that there are times when a doctor's consultation is in order. Emotional hurdles can arise from chemical imbalances in the brain or from other health and physical causes, not just experiential and spiritual sources. Our brain functions, hormones, and physiological makeup are as individual as our fingerprints. There are times when medical assistance will be helpful and necessary and should not be neglected out of embarrassment or fear of others' misunderstanding or disapproval. For very persistent and troubling emotional struggles that don't go away, it is strongly advised that a medical professional's evaluation be sought.

With or without a medical prescription, the principles in this book will help you become alert to destructive thinking patterns, show you practical and powerful ways to interrupt those patterns, and best of all, offer you freedom to more fully enjoy your life with refreshed understanding, perspective, and power.

2 Victory is Assured

I am expecting God to speak something meaningful to you because that's who He is, the living Word. He loves you and wants to bless you beyond your greatest expectations. He is pleased when you set aside other things and make listening to Him a priority. God has a wonderful way of speaking to our thoughts and emotions inwardly when we make the time to set aside pressing things and just be quiet and listen.

This takes some determination, as most of our lives are busy and noisy. Learn to enjoy quiet moments. It may be difficult at first, but it is a healthy habit you will enjoy as you practice it. Make a cup of tea and find a comfortable chair. I used to find my quiet time in the bathtub because my family wouldn't bother me there.

Sometimes I even filled it with water! Just find a time and place where you won't have distractions or interruptions.

When we detect the sinister slither of negative emotions, we will take on the challenge. We will be courageous, face our personal set of facts, and determine to choose a godly, victorious mind-set. God is all about victory! We're not going to run or hide when we encounter difficult inner battles. We're not going to let unresolved things fester in our emotions and spirits. Instead, we will deal with the upsets. By doing so, we are truly upending the devil, and short-circuiting the enemy's plan to kill our joy, steal our peace, and destroy our faith. You can be sure God is on your side for this battle!

On any battleground, the first strategy is to identify the enemy. It is easy to overlook this, regarding our inner lives where our thoughts and emotions form. It is imperative to recognize the enemy and identify the source of conflict. Sometimes it is obvious; but most of the time the enemy is sneaky, underhanded, subtle and hiding out, hoping not to be uncovered. Our emotions are vulnerable to subversive tactics. We can go along in our routines, feeling it is a "normal" day, when we have unwittingly accepted our unsettled thoughts or emotions as normal—for us. It may have been normal in the sense of usual, but it is not the best normal we are meant to enjoy.

So we must be alert to what is happening in our minds, expose the source, and devise a strategy to combat it and defeat it. In each chapter, a plan will emerge for dealing with specific and common emotional battles. I can tell you they have helped people in all kinds of situations, and they will help you. Not because I have developed a new whiz-bang-best-ever-solution-for-all-things snake oil. They work because they are the plan of God for His children, and they are empowered by the Holy Spirit to accomplish it. With the unmatched power of the God of the universe behind you, you will experience victory, one day at a time, while new habits and strengths develop. "For no word from God will ever fail." (Luke 1:37 NIV)

You may read the words I write and think about them in a completely different context, substituting your own experiences, rather than the examples I give. That is good. The Holy Spirit will call to your attention what He wants you to think about. Don't worry about trying to explain it to anyone else. What's important is that you heard it in your spirit. It is real and it is meant just for you.

This book is intended to be somewhat interactive. You will have opportunities to think about your specific situation and make a plan based on God's principles concerning your challenges. In this respect, it is a kind of working journal. I have sprinkled Scriptures liberally throughout, because I am thoroughly convinced God's Word is where the power is for transformation of our thoughts and our lives. Without His words, I am only another voice among thousands of others, and have little to offer for lasting changes.

At the end of each chapter are pertinent Bible scriptures for you to read, reread, and contemplate. They will soon become an anchor for your thoughts, and a refreshing wind to blow away false concepts and persistent thoughts that rob you of your peace of mind. There are also questions in each chapter and steps for you to take that will reveal your thinking, identify possible influences, and help you plan a workable strategy to free yourself from unproductive thoughts and emotions that distract and disturb you.

The goal is victory. The word *victory* often conjures up images of trophies and medals and ceremonies and awards. These are all exciting and good, but usually those shining achievements go to only a few—the top dogs, the talented, the stand-out achievers. A real victory is a much more powerful and lasting kind. We don't have to keep it dusted off and shined up. It is stored in our inner being and is achievable by every one of us, not just a select few!

These meaningful victories are usually noticed by us before anyone notices the change. It is like a secret pact between you and God. He knows those bothersome emotions and thinking patterns have plagued you and drained your energies. Some of them nag at you constantly, like a backstage prompter. Others even boldly take the spotlight front and center. They are audaciously persistent. A few show up only periodically with varying degrees of intensity. Whether they are constant or intermittent, negative thoughts and emotions steal your joy, rob your peace, and erode your faith. That is not the abundant life Jesus spoke of when He said, "I came to give you life, and life more abundantly." Because Jesus clearly stated that He came to give you life, and an abundant life at that, I can assure you that overcoming things that hinder your life is His plan for you! God will be at work in you and for you as you give your "Mission Impossible" to God for His powerful work in your life.

There are things, events, and people in our lives that we have no control over. Losses and upsets come to us through death, divorce, deception, financial mistakes, aging, illness, accidents, and many other uncontrollable circumstances. But as someone said, "Life is not what happens to you. Life is about what you do with what happens to you." It's not about actions as much as it's about reactions. It is not, "Why God, did you let this happen to me?" It is "Now that this has happened to me, God, what do you want me to do?"

Isn't it strange how one moment everything seems rosy, then—POW!—something happens to upset the tranquility?! Where does the turmoil come from? Not from God, unless He is giving us a lesson in discernment between God-appointed opportunities and human-created chaos! A good guiding principle for making choices is to remember God is not the author of confusion or strife. In fact, He will take confusion and strife and show us wondrous things about Himself when we give all control to Him and seek His will in the situation. Handing God the controls is the best First Step for each emotional battle we face. Subsequent practical steps for each challenge will be given in each chapter, specific things you can do for what bothers you most.

God wants to speak to us, to comfort us, encourage us, and to give us His perspective. He wants to enable us to identify and face those people, that event, or a certain circumstance, and emerge victorious with strength and peace of mind. Sounds like a tall order? It is, but God delights in doing what seems impossible to us. He is marvelous in the way He takes on those things that we cannot handle on our own. "With man this is impossible, but not with God. All things are possible with God." (Mark 10:27) That is good news. When I have tried and

19

failed, God readily comes to my aid with His show of strength in spite of my inability. Nothing is impossible with God. Sometimes it is instantaneous with an "Aha!" moment. But usually it is a process. It is always a transformation of my thinking and my perspective— letting go of my preconceived ideas and biases, recognizing the source, receiving God's way of looking at things, and responding through the power of His Holy Spirit. It takes time, and it takes attention. You are giving it time and attention. You are on the road to freedom and transformation.

As we proceed, I recommend jotting down "aha" moments that the Lord brings to your mind. There is space at the end of each chapter for you to do this. You will find it useful later when you want to think some more about something He impressed upon you. Or record a particularly helpful scripture. Or an analogy. God speaks in many ways! Writing down insights, thoughts, or prayers is highly recommended by counselors and therapists. It is wonderful the things that are brought forth from the spirit when we slow down long enough to reflect and jot down things for reminders or future thinking times. There will be some patterns that will emerge to give you insight and help you deal with those troubling thoughts and emotions that you want to be rid of.

"Therefore, do not be conformed to this world, but be transformed by the renewing of your mind." (Romans 12:2) Transformation can happen. Our minds can be renewed and be transformed to affect our thinking, behaviors, and infuse our lives with more beauty and peace. Who doesn't want that?

You may have had quite a battle today, getting through the day's tasks, the unexpected happenings, and solving everyone's proclaimed emergency. Maybe you feel guilty, taking this time for yourself, away from others' expectations and your usual responsibilities. If you suspect you have an overactive need to fix things and make everyone happy, let it be the perfect introduction to correcting an overactive negative emotion that commonly plagues wonderful, responsible, conscientious people—hyper-responsibility.

"Thanks be to God who gives us the victory through our Lord Jesus Christ." (1 Corinthians 15:57)

3 Hyper-Responsibility

Caring Christians with a soft heart, compassion, and the gift of mercy are most vulnerable to hyper-responsibility. Hyper means "overactive." Our spirit of lovingkindness is from the Holy Spirit. But it must be guided by the Holy Spirit to be expressed and acknowledged appropriately. If it is in your sweet nature to rush to help whenever you see or hear of a need, you are vulnerable to hyper-responsibility. And that often leads to extra stress in your life. Like many good things, responsibility can be misunderstood and misapplied. Because we care about others, it is easy to feel overly responsible for everyone's happiness. Sometimes we are called people pleasers.

Another term is *enabler*, identified and addressed by Al Anon, the support program for friends and families of alcohol abusers. The program describes well-meaning persons who want to make life good and pleasant for everyone. In many ways people-pleasers have an unselfish drive, but it can be twisted by the enemy to become an unbalanced perception of one's actual responsibilities and life purpose. Living without recognizing this will inevitably cause well-meaning helpers to feel overwhelmed or guilty, or both.

How is this possible? People-pleasers want everyone to be happy, and they go to great lengths to try to achieve that by giving in to unreasonable expectations, avoiding confrontation, and allowing others to pursue unwise actions, attitudes, and behaviors to the detriment of themselves or others. Of course we are to think of others, provide needs when appropriate, encourage, help, and support. Good is done when it is balanced and wisely applied. But people-pleasers do not realize that their concentrated determination to keep things running smoothly all the time for everyone, no matter what, is actually providing an unhealthy environment for others to take unfair advantage of their soft hearts.

People-pleasers and enablers also do not realize we are diminishing our own capabilities and confidence each time we give in to pressure that goes against what we believe is a better thing or a better time. Pleasers often postpone their own talents and abilities because they feel it is best to do for someone else first. Unfortunately, there are many "do this first for someone else" events, and the personal needs and expressions of the pleaser get sidelined repeatedly, and perhaps never even addressed. By constantly ignoring or postponing our own gifts and true responsibilities that God has given us, we neglect the spiritual purpose and meaningful plan that God has designed for us. The apostle Paul urges in his letter to Timothy, "Do not neglect the gift that is in you."

This reminds us that we have spiritual gifts that God has placed in us to use for His purposes. Each of us is a special design of God, placed on earth for such a time as this, to be a part of God's great purpose. We have been given gifts that are meant to bless others, to cooperate with God's kingdom purposes, which will allow us to grow in God's grace, all for His glory. When we give inordinate attention to pleasing others and neglect the abilities, talents, and skills we are meant to use, we are surrendering opportunities to serve in God's kingdom.

We end up wondering why we feel so exhausted, unsatisfied, and frustrated. We don't realize that while we are working hard to serve someone else's demands or expectations just to keep the peace or avoid disagreement, we are not drawing on the strength and provision of the Holy Spirit. We are acting in the flesh (human way of thinking) and undermining God's greater purpose. Paul reminds us, don't be hyperactive people-pleasers; do your work to please God, keeping His greater purpose in mind.

"Slaves, in all things obey those who are your masters on earth, not with external service, as those who merely please men, but with sincerity of heart, fearing the Lord. Whatever you do, do your work heartily, as for the Lord rather than for men, knowing that from the Lord you will receive the reward of the inheritance. It is the Lord Christ whom you serve." (Colossians 3:22-24 NASB) When we have the conscious awareness that whatever we do we are serving Christ, it puts things into perspective to be choosey about our tasks and our time.

Of course we want others to be happy and comfortable, to feel valued. This is putting others ahead of our own desires, and that is an unselfish Christian trait. But there are some slippery aspects that can infiltrate and infect the people-pleaser's thinking. Part of a desire to please others may be that we need and value their approval above other important considerations. But at what cost? Balancing considerations are: What is the best way? What is the overall need? Is a greater purpose being set aside to accommodate the immediate demand? What other things must go by the wayside in order to accommodate the request? Is quality being compromised? Is character being compromised? These are good reminders which suggest a strong caution to think through the reasons we respond to others and their demands. Whom am I trying to please? And why? I had better think about it. Possibilities are:

1. It makes me feel good because I see myself as a good person, giving up my own desires in order to satisfy someone else. I have to check my motives: Is this a pleasant feeling of martyrdom? Is it a misguided massaging of personal pride?

2. It makes the other person happy, and so I don't have to deal with their disapproval. Check motives: Is it to avoid conflict? Am I insecure in defending my position? Am I lacking self-confidence?

3. I feel coerced into agreement, and then resent it. This is a clue that the motive for acting agreeably came from a fleshly human motive, not a God-inspired one.

4. I value what someone else thinks more than I value my physical and emotional health. (Worrying over

things in the middle of the night, losing sleep, and feeling stressed all the time is not healthy!)

5. I think I am indispensable. This is a prideful attitude and does not honor God. I check my attitude by considering what they would do 50 years from now when I am not around! Answer? They will find someone else! And hmmm,… I'm not indispensable.

6. I am willing to give up something I know God has asked of me, in order to please this person instead of God. Giving up God-given opportunities deprives me of the blessings that accompany God's work through me. Do I really want that?

Please consider these deceptive influences as you carefully think over possible reasons you allow yourself to be pulled into scenarios that you later regret. A key to overcoming negative emotions is defining the issues and their underlying influences, so take all the time you need to do a thorough and honest self-assessment.

Consider this hypothetical scenario:

Wanda and Geraldine are working on a group project to open a little café that will raise money for a charity. Wanda has been working like a beaver for many days to help get things ready for the opening. She has baked an assortment of pastries, sent out invitations, and written articles for the local newspaper and magazine inserts. Adding these to her usual responsibilities at her church, at home, and taking care of her aging parent, Wanda is ready to be done with her obligations on the café project. She is relieved she can see the finish line.

Geraldine admires Wanda because she knows that Wanda is reliable, hard-working, caring, and efficient. She feels the deadline approaching and needs someone to take care of the last minute painting and decorating. She anxiously brings her difficulty to Wanda, asking her to work on the final task of decorating the tables in the café.

Wanda has had her hands full and isn't happy about weaving anything new into her tightly packed schedule. Wanda also knows that artistic designs and decorations are not her strength. She wants to help, but is feeling worn out from lack of sleep because of tending to her mother's needs at night. She turns down Geraldine's plea for help.

Geraldine is not happy. She tells her, "But Wanda, I know you can do a great job. I always count on you. It's just a little café, and we need to get it open for business next week."

Wanda tries to be more polite in her words than what is going on in her head. "I'm sorry, Geraldine, but I just can't take on any new projects. I'm sure there will be someone else who can do that better than I can. I'm not very artistic and don't really have a good sense of color and design."

Geraldine continues to pressure her, until tears well up in Wanda's eyes. Wanda turns away and says, "I just can't, Geraldine. I'm sorry."

Geraldine notices the tremble in Wanda's voice and smiles inwardly. She thinks, "I'll just ask her again tomorrow. She will give in. She always does. I'll tell her I can't find anyone else to help." To begin her undercover manipulating, and make her point to Wanda, Geraldine puts her hands on her hips and sniffs, "Well, I really thought I could count on you, Wanda."

Poor Wanda. She is being unfairly punished by Geraldine only because she recognizes her limitations, and has to reluctantly say, "No." All she can think of is how disappointed and angry Geraldine is with her. And she doesn't know how to fix it. She may give in tomorrow.

When I think back on my younger years, with life so full of taking care of home and family, volunteering in my kids' classrooms, volunteering for church and community projects, (and don't even mention the job and holidays!), it makes me tired just thinking about it now! Guess what? It made me tired then, too! It was really hard for me to "just say no" because I saw the value in the project I was being asked to do. It would help someone. I had the skill to do it. They needed someone who would complete the task. So I caved in, agreed, and staggered from one round of activities to the next round with only brief interludes of sanity before the next obligation. I'm sure I was playing into my own cleverly disguised ugly sin of pride, thinking I, only I, could adequately (no, wait—marvelously) fill the need. After all, I was the one they asked, wasn't I? I felt needed and important.

There will always be more to do than there is time for. Our challenge is to determine which of the tasks are those God has for us, versus which are just requests for help because someone needs to fill a slot and put a "Done" check mark next to an item on their To-Do List. Discerning the difference, we can make better choices to use our time without wearing ourselves out. It is an ongoing process, determining what's what. Just because it's a good thing doesn't mean it's your good thing to do. It takes wisdom and prayer to know whether to take on added responsibilities.

Instead of thinking about our availability only, we should also think of someone else who could be involved. Sometimes by refusing a task, we are opening the door for someone else to be blessed—someone who wants to be involved but wasn't offered the opportunity because we were too busy jumping in. Just because we have done it before, we must not think we are the only ones who can do the job. When we decline a task, we may be blessing some shy person who is longing to do the very thing we are grumpily agreeing to and wish we didn't have to do.

It helps me to know that when we are short on wisdom, God tells us to ask for it, and He will give it. (James 1:4) And immediately, any time, we can ask Him. We have prayer available to us. The challenge is to set aside other things for the moment and take the time to pray, ask God, then wait quietly for what He impresses upon our thoughts and emotions.

I have found it's helpful to make lists of the Pros and Cons involved in decisions. This helps me to sort out my thoughts, and I use this strategy frequently. Then I can consider the request in light of what I believe God is showing me about my time, energy, and talents. Ask for strength to resist the urge—yours or the urging of others—when it is not God who is doing the urging.

Scripture talks about burden-bearing. It is fascinating that two opposing instructions appear in the same passage

"Bear one another's burdens." And "Each one must bear his own burden." (Galatians 6:1-5) They sound like contradictions. But there are two different words in the original language that were translated into the same English word, "burden."

The first word for "burden" was translated from the original word meaning "boulder," a huge burden that is too heavy for one person alone to carry or move. That boulder-size burden is the burden we are told to help others carry. These are the burdens that are attitudes and events that shake us to the core. No need to describe the type of burden. We know them when they are weighing us down to the extent we feel we cannot take another breath without counsel and help of some kind. It is appropriate to ask for a fellow burden-bearer in these cases. And it is, of course, appropriate to come alongside another who needs your encouragement, your prayers, and any practical help you can give to help shoulder such a load from one who is on the verge of collapse.

The second word for burden is a different-size burden. It is likened to a "knapsack," the size you would carry your lunch in, with a few other items. Lightweight, easy to carry, a possession belonging to the one who carries it. These manageable problems and challenges, faults, and difficulties that come into our daily lives are the lightweight burdens we are to carry on our own. We are to be responsible and mature, and figure out with God's help the best way to manage them. They contribute to our growth as individuals and as followers of Christ.

It helps to have a clear distinction in mind between the two types of burdens when we are asked to take on a

31

new task. Sometimes we have no choice about boulder-sized burdens. We must care for an aging parent, or a sick family member. Or perhaps we ourselves have failed miserably and need spiritual restoration. Maybe a friend calls in tears, begging for a listening ear. A neighbor has a traumatic event, creating a need for food or shelter or some other sudden necessity that we must tend to. We are called upon to love not only in words, but also in deed. These boulder burdens usually show up unexpectedly, and we move things in our schedules to make time for such heavy events.

It is primarily the "knapsack" variety that this chapter is about, when we take on burdens that are meant for someone else to carry. If you are an habitual burden-bearer, become alert to the knapsack burden, the lighter one, that the owner can and should carry on her/his own. You have yours. I have mine. Don't feel pressured to take on others' burdens that were not meant for you to carry. I like the warning sign I saw in a workshop:

ATTENTION:
Procrastination on your part
does not constitute an emergency on my part.

The sign is a reminder that I need to carry my own burden, take care of my responsibilities in a timely way, and not thrust them upon others, expecting them to pick up the pieces of my irresponsible management.

We have our own knapsacks to carry. However, even a knapsack can become overloaded if we keep adding small items, one after another. There comes a time when the seams of our burden-bearing knapsacks begin to strain and split, and we realize we have packed too much to carry. Each item in the knapsack seems so small when we add it to our bag; that is the sneaky factor. People hasten to tell us, "It is just a small request. It won't take much time." It is hard to tell others that we can't accept "just one more little item" to carry even though we want to help them out, because it looks (to them) like such a small request.

However, it is important to remember that all these little items add weight. A number of "little" rocks rested on a scale can equal the weight of one unmanageable boulder. Take time to consider the weight and meaning of the burden you have been asked to share with someone. Is God asking you to carry it? Or is it one about which your inner voice whispers, "It is too much for me right now. Listen. Don't take it on. It can be done without my involvement." It is not up to you to personally solve every person's problems, or carry every burden that you hear about, even though the first inclination of your heart may want to.

As you begin to differentiate between these two very different types of burdens, you will start to feel relieved of extra responsibilities you have been gathering up into your own knapsack. Your shoulders will feel relaxed and your heart will be lighter. You will discover some "burdens" can be left with their rightful owner. You do not have to bear manageable burdens that are in someone else's knapsack.

It will take some time to remember and practice these principles, and you will probably take on some burdens that you will afterwards realize with regret were not yours to carry. Don't despair. It is part of the learning process, and you will see more clearly for the next time. As you begin to practice discernment and take charge of your time and energy, you will find new confidence and freedom to enjoy tasks that are truly yours, ones that were designed for you and that you are equipped to do.

While I was learning to do this, I received a great suggestion that I have used over the years. When you feel put on the spot and can't quickly think how to say "No" at the time, just say, "I need to think about it and get back to you with an answer." You don't have to give an immediate answer. This gives you time to think it through, pray about it, and decide exactly how you want to say "no" with grace and confidence if that's what you need to do.

A simple answer could be, "I would like to help you out, but I just cannot do that right now." You do not have to give a reason. The fact that you "do not feel able to do that now" is a reasonable answer that should be accepted. If further information is demanded, hold firm and repeat, "I'm sorry, I really wish I could help you out, but I just am not able to do it this time." Repeat it again if you are pressed further.

It is the "broken record" method of letting others know you can't do what they are asking. After a while, they will be more tired of hearing your answer than you are of repeating it. It releases you of having to give further explanations, which sometimes only adds to the stress. Sometimes an extended explanation opens the door for the requester to argue and break down your initial wise decision. We people-pleasers often make it more complicated than it needs to be. A courteous, respectful person will accept your answer even if they are disappointed by it. A discourteous, disrespectful person who doesn't accept your answer is not someone you need to please. It is not someone you will want to have lunch with next week for a long, leisurely, confidential communication about meaningful things.

You are not obligated to keep any person happy by sacrificing your peace of mind and giving up time that God wants you to use for other purposes. He has arranged other things on your timetable including time to rest, to recreate, or to do something for yourself for your own mental health. These are God-given gifts to refresh you and give you time for inspiration. Even Jesus took time to get away from the crowds to pray and get direction from His father. Give yourself permission to take time to rest. Schedule it in if you must. When you are asked to do something at a time you have set aside for rest or recreation, it is truthful and perfectly acceptable to say, "I'm sorry, but that day is already scheduled for something else."

Doing this, you may encounter a guilty feeling. It is false guilt, another sneaky negative emotion that needs to be exposed and defeated. False guilt is the subject of the next chapter.

QUESTIONS:

1. What are your strengths? What God-given gifts do you have that bring joy to yourself and others when you are exercising them?

2. What are your weaknesses? What kinds of tasks frustrate you and drain your energy?

3. What are your priorities at this time of your life? Career? School? Marriage? Children? Grand-children? Volunteer work? Growing in faith? Building new habits? Church ministry? Learning?

4. How much time will you set aside to allow yourself to work on your priorities?

5. What kinds of demands cause you to feel obligated, rather than cheerful about them?

6. Create a statement now, in advance, for the next time you are being pressured to take on a job or do a favor for someone when you aren't ready for it. Write it below so you are ready to use it when the need arises.

STEPS:

1. Think about the request, whether it is in your realm of talents and skills.

2. Consider the time factor involved.

3. Don't quickly or automatically accept additional responsibilities. Think about why you may or may not want to add the task to your busy schedule.

4. Think about if your acceptance of the task is simply to avoid being thought of in a lesser way.

5. Consider what things you may be forfeiting by using your time for this task.

6. Remind yourself that pleasing God is the overall measurement of success.

7. Consider the season of life you are in. Some seasons offer more time, or less time and energy to take on extra tasks. Be forgiving of yourself if you feel you cannot help out on a worthy cause.

PERTINENT SCRIPTURES:

"Whatever you do, do it heartily as for the Lord rather than for men." Colossians 3:23 NASB

"But if any of you lacks wisdom, let him ask of God, who gives to all generously and without reproach, and it will be given to him." James 1:5 NASB

"But each one has his own gift from God, one in this manner and another in that." 1 Corinthians 7:7

"As each one has received a gift, minister it to one another, as good stewards of the manifold grace of God." 1 Peter 4:10

"So let each one give as he purposes in his heart, not grudgingly or of necessity; for God loves a cheerful giver." 2 Corinthians 9:7

4 False Guilt

As we begin to get a handle on hyper-responsibility, and learn to say "no" to excessive or unreasonable requests, we become more able to recognize our valuable God-given responsibilities apart from the demands and expectations of others. When we respond to our true God-given priorities, we find new energy and joy in the tasks and ministries that God has gifted us for. However, as we develop more confidence and assertiveness, we sometimes experience negative reactions from those who previously leaned on us for their convenience and an easy answer. This is why we should take a look at false guilt and learn to identify it.

First, let's think about legitimate guilt. Guilt is an emotion that God allows us to feel in order to show us our error and need for repentance. True guilt is a blessing. Through our sense of wrongfulness and guilt, we are disappointed in ourselves, perhaps even repulsed, to the point we seek God's forgiveness. This is godly repentance, leading to our salvation and refining our new walk of faith. "When we confess our sins, God is faithful to forgive us our sins and to cleanse us from all unrighteousness." (John 1:5-6) God allows us to feel shame and guilt to the extent that we desire to turn away from the sin and its discomfort and innate destructiveness.

Careful reading of Jesus' words relieves us of guilt after we are saved. When Jesus says, "I came not to condemn the world, but that the world might be saved," we read it and believe it. Paul asserts, "There is now no condemnation to those who are in Christ." (Romans 5:1) When we have surrendered our lives to Christ, we are free from condemnation and guilt. Jesus Christ bore the burden and penalty for our sins, and we are no longer held guilty for them. God told us so.

So, why then do I feel guilty when I disappoint someone? As we discussed in the previous chapter on hyper-responsibility and people-pleasing, the "guilt" I feel may be misplaced and mislabeled. Think it through. Don't accept a bad feeling without evaluating its legitimacy. Instead of drowning in a flood of murky misery, I must prevent the inevitable round of self-inflicted accusations I am subject to, and throw myself a life-preserver. I must slow down, take time, and ask myself,

"Have I done anything that is actually wrong?"

"Have I deliberately or accidentally caused harm in any way?"

"Have I disobeyed God in anything I said or did?"

40

If I'm unsure about my self-evaluation, I can ask a trusted friend who will help me with a mature and honest answer. If the answer to these questions is an honest "no," then what I am feeling is not God-given guilt. It is actually false guilt. The devil uses false guilt to throw a pall of self-condemnation over our freedom and joy in Christ. It's imperative to recognize it for what it really is—it is false.

Discernment is needed. If there has been a transgression, it is true guilt and I need to confess it, seek forgiveness, and make restitution as needed. But I am not meant to wallow in remorse and guilt for things that have been confessed and forgiven. They are to be put behind me so that I move forward in faith. The devil hopes I will not remember any of that. He wants to make me believe I am an exception, that something was too bad to be forgiven by God and that I am unacceptable to Him. That, of course, is a lie from the father of lies, and must not be given any credibility at all. "We are accepted in the Beloved!"

"… having predestined us to adoption as sons by Jesus Christ to Himself, according to the good pleasure of His will, to the praise of the glory of His grace, by which He made us accepted in the Beloved. In Him we have redemption through His blood, the forgiveness of sins, according to the riches of His grace." (Ephesians 1:5-7)

In the previous chapter's example, Wanda was already up to her ears, helping and serving. She obviously has a heart to be helpful and has proven it by her generous involvement in getting the coffee shop ready with cookies, posters, and a multitude of kitchen duties. But because Geraldine is upset that she wouldn't help with decorating the coffee shop, Wanda is suffering with a sense of guilt. It is false guilt because Wanda has done nothing wrong. In fact, she has done quite the opposite. Wanda has given generously of her time and talents to the extent that she has no more time available! And, besides, decorating is not her forte!

It would have been frustrating and probably failure-prone for Wanda to take on decorating the coffee shop. She realized that, and "just said no." But because Geraldine didn't show grace and understanding, Wanda's emotions took a tumble. The reason she felt bad was because Geraldine was disappointed, not because she had done anything wrong.

Sometimes we fall prey to taking on someone else's problems and making them our own when they really have nothing to do with us. It is only the result of the person putting pressure on us with many arguable reasons why we should fulfill the request, even after we have declined. It is a kind of manipulation. If we don't pause long enough to figure this out, we fall prey to false guilt.

Compassionate and caring people want to meet others' needs, solve problems, and make life easier for others. It is hard to let go of trying to make all of life better for everyone. No one is equipped to do that, except God. And no one should become burdened by unrealistic expectations. Solving everyone's problems is not a burden God lays upon our shoulders. We spent time thinking about this in the previous chapter. If you need to, review your thoughts on hyper-responsibility. False Guilt is a recipe for defeat that the devil specializes in mixing up. Here's how the recipe works:

False Guilt Deluxe

Take one tender person with a heart to serve.
Add 6 cups of good intentions and lots of hard work.
Sprinkle with accusations and misunderstandings.
Beat thoroughly.
Put all ingredients in pressure cooker.
Stir to mix ingredients thoroughly.
Add seasonings: time pressure, perfectionism, desire
to please, unrealistic expectations, self-condemnation,
manipulation from others, demonic whispers.

Cover tightly.
Turn up the heat. Keep the heat on. Do NOT lift the
lid until completely overdone!

Okay, so you recognize the scenario and even can personalize it with your own experience. So can I. I very recently had this experience. You may have experienced it in your family, your friends, or at your work place. It happens.

There is initial shock and dismay when we realize that our good efforts and good intentions have been

43

misunderstood, and even criticized. We wonder, "How could they think such a thing!"

There is denial. "I don't think they really said that." "They couldn't have thought that." "That is so contrary to what really happened."

There is sadness. "I feel really, really, really, really sad that our relationship is damaged."

There is confusion. "What did I do wrong to cause this misunderstanding?"

And then the devil plays his trump card. False guilt. "It's my fault that they are upset. I should have said it this way." Or, "If only I had done it differently."

Sometimes, in truth, our actions are not the primary cause. People have expectations and they respond in unexpected ways. We can't anticipate every reaction or attitude that crops up. We can't avoid every problem, even if we anticipate them. And we can't always make it better, no matter how much we want to. Like Wanda thought to herself, "I don't know how to fix it."

False guilt is an insidious tool the devil uses to steal our peace, kill our joy, and destroy our faith. It is so subtle. We actually unwittingly sabotage ourselves. It happens when we inadvertently substitute what others think of us for what God thinks of us. We focus on what others are saying, even when they are, um... wrong. Even unjust accusations can trigger false guilt. For this reason, unjust accusations and the complicating emotions that accompany them is the subject of the next chapter.

Satan knows our triggers, and those will be where he concentrates his efforts to set us off! I have had a few triggers tickled this week, myself. Triggers are different for each one of us. But they have the same evil purpose: to trip us up, to get us off balance spiritually, to upset us emotionally, to interfere with relationships, and to cause us to doubt God's love and goodness. This is the enemy's subtle attack against our faith and the abundant life Jesus came to give us. Remember Jesus said, "I have come that they might have life and have it more abundantly."

There is another subtle undercurrent to false guilt and the way we berate ourselves for things that were not of our creation. That undercurrent is one I detected in myself when I realized why I felt bad about disappointing someone. I felt bad because I knew I had lost a level of good standing with that person. Losing their admiration, I actually felt the sting of wounded pride. This was a revelation to me!

First of all, I didn't know I had that disguised Pride lurking in there. Second, I didn't realize that my compulsion to please others was rooted in Pride. I just didn't want anyone to think badly of me, because, after all, I was a pretty fine person. I wanted them to hold me in high esteem. Yep. That's pride. Granted, we desire to have a good reputation. We want to reflect God's goodness and love to others. Those are good things. But for me, those were not the reasons I was feeling bad about disappointing someone.

I felt bad for the wrong reason. I wasn't concerned about reflecting God's glory and goodness. I was concerned about me. I wanted to reflect my own glory and goodness. This is hard to write, just as it was hard to admit to myself when the Holy Spirit pointed it out to me. It is sneaky. Once it is exposed, though, it is liberating. It alerts me now when I'm feeling false guilt over something. I have to ask myself, "Why am I feeling bad about this when I didn't do anything wrong?" It's probably wounded pride, a slip in my exalted self-image or someone else's perceived image of me. The Spirit reminded me "not to think more highly of yourself than you ought."

Lord God, this is my prayer: Give me patience to endure. You are worth it all. Now perfect, establish, strengthen, and settle me through Your truth. Give me discernment to separate truth from lies. Thank You for your powerful Word and the promises of Your faithfulness to uphold Your children. Thank you for giving me discernment and victory over false guilt. In Jesus' Name and for His glory. Amen.

Contemplate the questions below. Allow the Holy Spirit to settle and illuminate your thinking and bring you answers.

QUESTIONS:

1. What sort of experience (or person) creates a sense of false guilt in you?

2. How can you know the difference between feeling false guilt and real guilt over something that needs to be confessed and forgiven?

3. What truth will help you avoid getting caught up in false guilt?

4. What will you do to refocus your thoughts and fortify yourself against false guilt in the future?

STEPS:

1. Identify the source of the conflict. Ask God if you are feeling guilty because of sinning against Him or anyone else. That's important. Wait. Listen for His reassurance. Be open to His correction. But also be open to His reassurance. Let godly others help you sort through the process if you're not sure how to discern between God's truth and false guilt in your situation.

2. Ask yourself, "What am I really feeling bad about?" Myself? Disobeying God? Or losing stature in someone else's perception?

3. Make sure you are not feeling guilty over an earlier situation and are transferring that feeling to the current issue. Don't take on something to try to make an earlier problem go away.

4. Remember, above all, that Christ has forgiven you of all confessed sin; so reliving guilt for things already forgiven is FALSE guilt and is harassment from our enemy and the enemy of Christ. Resist it, by refusing to give it any time or thought energy.

5. Replace your nagging thoughts with scripture. Memorize an applicable verse and repeat it when guilt thoughts bombard you. Play or sing praise songs or hymns that refocus your attention on the love and greatness of God.

6. Realize God is at work in *all* that concerns you.

7. Trust Him and be patient, knowing God is pleased with you, even if others are not.

8. Pray until peace comes. Let others pray with you and for you. This is how we learn wisdom.

PERTINENT SCRIPTURES:

"This is the victory that overcomes the world, even our faith." 1 John 5:4

"For this purpose the Son of God came, to destroy the works of the devil." 1 John 3:8

"I have come that they might have life and have it more abundantly." John 10: 9-11

"God is not the author of confusion, but of peace." 1 Corinthians 14:13

"May the God of all grace, who called us to His eternal glory by Christ Jesus, after you have suffered a while, perfect, establish, strengthen, and settle you."
1 Peter 5:10

"For our struggle is not against flesh and blood, but against the rulers, against the authorities, against the powers of this dark world and against the spiritual forces of evil in the heavenly realms." Ephesians 6:11-13

"Whatever you do, do your work heartily, as for the Lord rather than for men, knowing that from the Lord you will receive the reward of the inheritance. It is the Lord Christ whom you serve." Colossians 3:23

"For God is not unrighteous to forget your work and labor of love, which you have shown toward His name, in that you have ministered to the saints, and do minister." Hebrews 6:10

"Let the word of Christ dwell in you richly." Colossians 3:16

"Faith comes by hearing and hearing the Word of God." Romans 10:17

5 Unjust Accusations

Unjust accusations hit with a force that is both unnerving and sinister. It is one thing to hit against something that is concrete and real. It is an entirely different thing to try to break through a wall that isn't real. Paul says, "Thus I fight: not as one who beats the air." (1 Corinthians 9:26)

Imagine trying to beat the air! That is what false accusations often feel like. There is nothing real to combat, so my fists can fly, and I can rant and scream, but it will make no difference, except to further frustrate and anger me, because there is nothing to land on! Unjust accusations are like that. They originate from a figment of someone's imagination, jumping to conclusions, gossip, outright lies, or a deliberate attempt to hurt someone regardless of their innocence.

There are persons who prefer to find things that justify their already-held opinions. They are not interested in knowing the whole story. They look for proofs for whatever they prefer to believe. These people are especially hard to appease or correct. You probably have tried to give pertinent facts about what you said or did, only to learn the person could not accept them even though they completely explained and clarified details that were clouding the issue.

It is exasperating and hurtful when our efforts to make amends only seem to solidify the accusatory thinking of the one we are talking to. You may be trying to overcome someone's unwarranted jealousy, prejudice, a misunderstanding, wrong interpretation, or an evil imagination of another person.

God knows all about unjust attacks against His children! He has given us revealing examples in His Word. One striking example is found in a New Testament story. Jesus is eating with His disciples, when Mary of Bethany comes to Him with a costly treasure, myrrh in an alabaster box. She breaks the box and pours out the expensive perfume on Jesus, anointing Him with it and with her tears. A disciple, Judas Iscariot, criticized her action, saying, "That valuable stuff could have been sold and given to the poor." Jesus shows He understands Mary's loving and sacrificial act. He defends her in the face of a wrong attitude and accusation! (This is especially noteworthy because the story is told in three of the four gospels: Mark, Matthew, and John). Jesus not only defends Mary for her sacrificial act. He also commends her and says she will be remembered forever for her devotion. And indeed she is. Read these accounts of Mary's lavish gift to fortify this truth in your mind. You will find it in Mark 14:3-9, Matthew 26:7-13, and John 12:3-8.

How comforting this is! When we are injured by unjust accusations and undeserved criticism, Jesus comes to our defense! Sometimes our efforts to make peace are rejected; in fact, they only seem to add fuel to the fire. Remember this: When the other side doesn't have ears to hear, it is not for us to carry the burden of explaining, correcting, and trying to fix things. We preserve our peace by leaving the argument in the hands of our heavenly Advocate, just as Jesus did. Look at His example, given to us in the gospels, and written about by Peter to suffering Christians.

In this portion of Scripture, Peter reminds us of the attitude that pleases God when we are faced with unfair treatment:

"Servants, be submissive to your masters with all respect, not only to those who are good and gentle, but also to those who are unreasonable. For this finds favor, if for the sake of conscience toward God a person bears up under sorrows when suffering unjustly. For what credit is there if, when you sin and are harshly treated, you endure it with patience? But if when you do what is right and suffer for it you patiently endure it, this finds favor with God." (1 Peter 2:18-23)

The reason such an attitude finds favor with God, is shown through Christ, our example. Peter explains in verse 21, "For you have been called for this purpose, since Christ also suffered for you, leaving you an example for you to follow in His steps, who committed no sin, nor was

53

any deceit found in His mouth; and while being reviled, He did not revile in return; while suffering, He uttered no threats, but kept entrusting Himself to Him who judges righteously."

It is a tremendous comfort to me to know that even if no one else understands the cause and details of my hurt and all it includes, JESUS does. He knows all things, sees each heart, and He is able to deal with the broken pieces. Each of us has certain ones around us who are more difficult to please than others. We can become distracted and distressed by occurrences of misunderstandings and false accusations. But we can be relieved of the harassment of those false voices by taking it to the righteous judge who knows they are false. He is the one who can turn bad things to good. God orchestrates things we cannot make happen.

He is the God of all truth and we can stake our lives on it.

Foundational Truth #1: Jesus sees it all, inside and out. He knows your heart. He knows what happened and what was said. He knows the truth of it all. He is your Advocate. He comes to your defense. There are things you cannot fix. There are things I cannot fix. But there is nothing HE cannot fix. It may not get fixed in the way we envision, but it will be His work, so it will be good.

I remember a time when my 4-year-old son came to me in tears with a broken toy. He was broken-hearted. It was his favorite toy and he couldn't fix it. My heart went out to him. I was happy to see that I could probably fix it easily. I took the toy in my lap and began to examine it.

My son, always interested in how things worked, leaned over to inspect it with me. His head was directly in my line of vision, and all I could see was his light brown hair. His little fingers were busily trying to reconnect the pieces while his tears flowed. The toy was completely invisible to me while he fiddled with the pieces in my lap. I gently nudged him to one side, saying, "I can fix it, Brian, but I can't see what I'm doing. Your head is in the way."

As I began putting the pieces back in place, there was that sweet head again, obscuring my vision of what my hands needed to do. I nudged him again, saying, "Honey, I can't see what I'm doing. Please move out of the way. Wait just a minute." This happened at least one more time. I was beginning to feel exasperated at his intense interest and involvement, which was interfering with my ability to help him. Finally, I distracted him with a task to do elsewhere and he moved away. I completed the repair then in short order. With his little fingers out of the way, it only took a few minutes. My little guy wanted so much to help, but his efforts only impeded the process.

I learned an important spiritual lesson through those few minutes. I thought of times that I bring my troubles, my broken things, to God and beg Him to help me. But I cannot let it alone. I have to "help" Him. I get in the way with my own efforts. Not because I think I know exactly what to do, but because I feel desperate to do something, anything, and I hope I can help out God.

I should remind myself that I already have done everything I know how to do, and none of it helped. Some patience and trusting would now be a better use of my time and energy.

55

It is good to want to solve a problem, to bring things to light about unjust accusations, but if I try to bring forth elements that others are not ready to accept, it only intensifies the frustration and anger on both sides. Some things require the passage of time before they will improve. Some things will develop in that passage of time to give illumination to the problem. Time often helps to show me some things about others or myself, what is true and what is not true, and how my faith is working, or isn't.

If I operate in my impatience, nothing gets fixed. I am in the way of God's work. My fleshly attempts to fix a spiritual issue won't get the job done. It must be done by the One who created all things, knows the heart of all persons, and sees the broken pieces. He alone knows how things fit together, and how it must be put together again. I can get in the way and slow down the whole process.

It is much better when I trust Him, and wait for Him to complete the process. My job is to get out of the way, pray, take comfort from His truth and His perfect knowledge and power, and wait. That's the hard part—to wait. Waiting for spiritual mending is just as important to the spiritual fixing process as it is to take a broken plastic toy, apply glue, hold the pieces together, and wait for the bonding. Trust the process that God is working while you wait. He is attentive to His children.

I am currently applying these principles. God has graciously sent me a distraction right now to keep me out of His way, to allow some necessary time to pass without me fussing over an unjust accusation from someone I care about very much. I am grateful that I do not have to spend every waking hour worrying about how to make reconciliation come about. I tried, and it fell on deaf ears for now. We do what we can, but life has better things for us than fussing and fuming over what we cannot fix. Some things can be repaired quickly. Other things take more time, and that rare commodity—patience.

Foundational Truth #2: Christ is at work in us to form us into His image. A big part of our needed formation is inner assurance that God is in full control, no matter how out of control things look or feel. Many works of the Spirit in us are done on our emotional landscape, scarred by injuries like false accusations which are some of the toughest situations that challenge us most. But He knows what to do with the incoming barrage, the flack, and the craters.

Foundational Truth #3: Christ is at work in others, too. Sometimes we have to step back and get out of the fray, and wait for others to fight their battles with God. When we refuse strife, God will take up the slack/cause. God knows each of His children need to grow to be more like Jesus, and He will accomplish His purposes. God always has a plan for everyone involved, believers or unbelievers. Perhaps my part in the conflict is to show the love of God to an unbeliever and to be a witness of His overcoming love and grace. To be a credible witness of it, I have to demonstrate it in real time with real people. Whether or not we see the results we hope for, it is God's will for us to bear patiently with unjust accusations and other offenses, as Christ did. This pleases God and strengthens our relationship with Him.

By the way, I heard a piece of advice many years ago that I've applied—when I can remember to do so—and it is worth solid gold. It goes like this: Wait three days. Most things are not an emergency and can wait three days. In three days, it is surprising how many things will be already worked out without our having to do anything at all. In waiting, we avoid impulsive actions and words, and give God time to work, including His work on our own attitudes and emotions! It gives us time to think and pray through areas of conflict and gain improved perspective.

Scripture says, "If at all possible, as much as depends on you, live peaceably with all men." We must do our part, and leave the rest to the Holy Spirit to handle. If our efforts to explain to someone who is imagining or twisting the facts do not achieve peace, we will preserve our own peace of mind only by handing it over to Christ, the only One who has complete access into the heart of each of us.

It is worth asking ourselves how important it really is to persuade the accuser of our innocence. Is it only for our own comfort? We cannot control what others do or say. But we can control how we react to it, inwardly, as well as outwardly. A spirit of malice will probably show up again, unless the accuser recognizes the damage done and whole-heartedly repents. We only have so much energy to expend trying to correct other people's misconceptions and lies. It can be a huge distraction, keeping us from more fruitful pursuits. Trying fruitlessly to prove our innocence and convince others of the same, prolongs the hurt and grieves the Holy Spirit.

Sometimes the wisest thing is to avoid such people, if at all possible. Paul, writing to the Ephesians, warned against tolerating maliciousness in any form. It stands to reason that keeping company with people who have these destructive habits is not advised, lest we take on their reprehensible habits:

"Let no corrupt word proceed out of your mouth, but only what is good for necessary edification, that it may impart grace to the hearers. And do not grieve the Holy Spirit of God, by whom you were sealed for the day of redemption. Let all bitterness, wrath, anger, clamor, and evil speaking be put away from you, with all malice. And be kind to one another, tenderhearted, forgiving one another, even as God in Christ forgave you." (Ephesians 4:29-32)

"Beloved, do not avenge yourselves, but rather give place to wrath; for it is written, 'Vengeance is Mine, I will repay,' says the Lord." (Romans 12:19)

Warren Wiersbe, in his Old Testament Commentary, wrote: "Life isn't easy, but if we submit to God's disciplines and let Him guide us in our decisions, we can endure the difficulties triumphantly and develop the kind of character that glorifies God."

Triumphant endurance is more than success. It is more than achievement. It is glorious, exuberant, winning, overcoming power! This is abundant life, triumphing over events and hurdles with power and grace that defies the world's expectations. We experience the power of God in us for our good and His glory. He works in us and for us and through us. What a wonder! We can be free from agonizing over false accusations when we believe God's promises and trust God for good outcomes, like Peter says as he wraps up his letter in 1 Peter 5:10, to suffering Christians:

"May the God of all grace, who called us to His eternal glory by Christ Jesus, after you have suffered a while, perfect, establish, strengthen, and settle you."

It is gloriously freeing when we take on the mind of Christ, leaving the results with Him who judges righteously. We become established, strengthened, and settled about things when we consciously remember that the Lord of the universe knows, cares, and is at work on our behalf. When our focus becomes pleasing Him, our God, "the things of earth become strangely dim in the light of His glory and grace," as the hymn goes. That is how we can leave false accusations in the dust, and go forward with a peaceful heart. The One who can really fix things, others, and even us, is on the job. He is able, wise, and loving. I will try to keep my busy hands out of the way of His work, and wait patiently for it all to settle out under His management.

But, do we believe this? If we have doubts, now is a perfect time to put it to the test. This leads us to inner victory: Instead of confusion…we can be fortified and inspired by scripture's dramatic examples.

Jesus was unjustly accused. He knew it was false, and He knew it was leading to His crucifixion. Yet, as Peter wrote: "when He suffered, He did not threaten, but committed Himself to Him who judges righteously." (1 Peter 2:23)

And "Therefore let those who suffer according to the will of God commit their souls to Him in doing good, as to a faithful Creator."(1 Peter 4:19)

"And whatever you do, do it heartily, as to the Lord and not to men, knowing that from the Lord you will receive the reward of the inheritance; for you serve the Lord Christ. But he who does wrong will be repaid for what he has done, and there is no partiality." (Colossians 3:23-25)

This is a new focus. A God focus. An inner triumph focus. As we begin to see things from God's perspective, we grow in the fruits of the Spirit which include long-suffering and self-control. And although Scripture reassures us we will receive the reward of our inheritance, the benefits right now, today, are also rewarding. We have the ability to have a level of peace the world cannot know in the midst of turmoil. It may be quite a while before you see your injustice corrected. This is trying to faith. Instant results are what we prefer, but they generally are not what God ordains. He is more interested in growing us up into mature believers, with a faith refined like gold by repeated processing in refining fires.

You are discovering this book "ain't for sissies." I agree. These are hard issues. Matters of the heart that go against our natural inclinations are really tough ones. I have lived them. You probably have, too, because you are reading along with me. It is especially hard to let false accusations go undefended. Because they are unjust and we have a strong need to see justice play out, we are anxious to see justice in clear daylight. It usually takes time. But we are not the only people in history who have had to wait before seeing a satisfying ending. The Bible is full of such accounts. They let us know that we are not suffering because we have been singled out or set aside away from God's love. It is the human experience to deal with hard

61

things in life. God will bring us through. It is His desire to strengthen us in our faith and lead us into His good purposes for our lives.

Not everyone will see it through, especially after this chapter. The Lord is calling His people to get serious about this thing called faith. It is the same message He has been sending His people since the Garden of Eden. It is about relationship with God, about trusting Him. About believing Him and following Him, even when it doesn't seem to make sense to our natural minds. This is like tough love. I call it tough faith. Recognizing what must be done, and doing it. Believing it. Acting on it. Resolutely.

Christ is still wanting us to go forth and make disciples. In order to do that, we ourselves must become stronger disciples. That is what we are after, and no one said it would be easy. Easy, no. Rewarding, yes!

Letting go of old habits is not an easy task. It is more than passively letting go. It is grabbing them by the scruff of the neck and giving them a deliberate "Heave-Ho!" It is choosing to follow Jesus through the hard places in life, in the storms and in the wilderness, not just sailing placid seas with our fingertips trailing limply in the water. Jesus was honest with His disciples:

"Enter by the narrow gate; for wide is the gate and broad is the way that leads to destruction, and there are many who go in by it. Because narrow is the gate and difficult is the way which leads to life, and there are few who find it." (Matthew 7:13-14) Your willingness to follow Jesus through the narrow gate, through difficult situations and heartaches, entrusting it all to God, honors and glorifies your Savior. He sees and knows your heart. You are precious to Him. He eagerly comes alongside you to give you help and wisdom in your time of need.

QUESTIONS:

1. How important will this be five years from now? (Choose which battles are worth fighting.)

2. How much of your reaction is due to wounded pride?

3. As you pray about this, do you feel an appropriate freedom from wrong-doing? If so, take steps to let the anger or sadness go. God will fight your battle for you. Be patient.

4. Is there anything you need to do that you are not willing to do, to bring about peace with your accuser? Confess it to God, and let Him give you the strength to do what you know you should.

5. What can you do that will help preoccupy your thoughts? (Right brain activities are very effective. Creative things like music and art, or learning something new.)

STEPS:

1. Consider the source of the accusation. Take serious note, and let it be a learning experience for spiritual insight about human nature and how slyly the enemy tries to kill, steal and destroy, in any way possible.

63

2. Take time to contemplate the severity of the false accusations brought against Jesus. Compare them to the level of accusations against you. Ask God to put them into perspective for you.

3. Realize that Jesus did not let unjust criticism of Mary's lavish generosity go unnoticed. He took her side. He was her advocate. Jesus defended and commended her to his disciples. He comes alongside the humble follower. He is on your side.

4. Be patient. Wait for things to unfold. Expect to see God's amazing intervention on your behalf.

5. Trust God, knowing that He has the full story, knows your heart, and also the hearts of others who are involved. Take comfort in His approval of you. And leave the results with Him, who is the righteous judge of all men.

6. Know that you will receive the reward God intends for you. Your faith is more precious than gold to Him.

7. Choose scriptures that speak to you about this. Post them and memorize them. Repeat them to yourself and out loud to reinforce them in your thinking. Your emotions will follow their lead. Peace will replace your preoccupation.

PERTINENT SCRIPTURES:

"Stand still and see the salvation of the Lord which He will accomplish for you today." Exodus 14:13

"Therefore let the Lord be judge, and judge between you and me, and see and plead my case, and deliver me out of your hand." 1 Samuel 24:15

"He will make your innocence radiate like the dawn and the justice of your cause like the noonday sun." Psalms 37:6

"If God be for us, who can be against us?" Romans 8:31

"But if when you do what is right and suffer for it and you patiently endure it, this finds favor with God. For you have been called for this purpose, since Christ also suffered for you, leaving you an example for you to follow in His steps, who committed no sin, nor was any deceit found in His mouth; and while being reviled, He did not revile in return; while suffering, He uttered no threats, but kept entrusting Himself to Him who judges righteously." 1 Peter 4:18-23

(Jesus defends Mary against the unjust accusation of wasting her gift): "Truly I say to you, wherever the gospel is preached in the whole world, what this woman has done will also be spoken of in memory of her." Mark 14:6-9

"But thanks be to God, who always leads us in triumph in Christ." 2 Corinthians 2:14

"Do not be overcome by evil, but overcome evil with good." Romans 12:21

"God resists the proud but gives grace to the humble." 1 Peter 5:5

6 Discouragement and Depression

Depression is no fun. A really tough thing about depression is it is sometimes difficult to identify its origin. Sometimes the cause is obvious, such as when it follows a major traumatic event. But depression also can sneak up on us. It may begin with a small disappointment, leading to discouragement. When discouragement is prolonged or followed by a series of disappointing experiences, it can lead to bigger problems as accumulated emotions gather like a storm into a black cloud of depression.

Depression in varying degrees haunts us at different times in our lives. Sometimes it comes monthly with a change of hormones, a common experience for many women. That sense of depression fortunately is short-lived, but it is a miserable experience while it lasts. Sometimes an anniversary date comes that reminds us of a tragedy or loss. These are temporary things that can cause us to feel temporarily depressed.

But then there are big things that happen which contribute to prolonged feelings of hopelessness and helplessness. Many of us have had one or more such experiences. Death of a loved one, loss of job, false accusations, financial pressure, divorce, extended illness, betrayal, a bad report from a doctor. These and others are sizeable challenges to our faith.

Fortunately, God is not detached or uncaring about our pain. He has answers for us in all our experiences, from the smallest to the gigantic.

I am not speaking theoretically. I am speaking from experience. I'm going to give you the basic background in one paragraph, not belabor the point, because what's important in my story is the faithful provisions of God, not the circumstances that led up to them. It was a while ago, but the lessons learned are current, powerful, and valuable. I lost four precious loved ones within six months—my husband, my best friend and prayer partner, my father, and my grandmother. It was blow upon blow. I was teaching 4th grade at the time. I finished the school year in a fog, and decided I needed to change direction and go back to school for graduate studies.

I met a man who was an experienced and very successful con artist who presented himself as a devoted Christian. I fell for his charming deception and married him. This was when I learned just how subtle complete deception is. So very subtle, until it has you in its clutches. It was a miserable but valuable experience, teaching me much about demonic ways that masquerade as acceptable, even admirable. I want you to know that God intervened wonderfully, revealing the truth of my situation with clarity in less than a year. I filed for annulment of the marriage on the basis of fraud and the annulment was granted.

Why do I bring this up? Because although the evil influences and environment were removed, the emotional debris in my heart, spirit, and mind remained piled up like rubble in a war zone. I struggled to work through disappointment in myself, disillusionment, financial losses, and deceptions. It was a long time before relief came. During the waiting time, longing for relief, I suffered common elements of depression—sleeplessness, loneliness, and even times with dear friends that were sometimes difficult. I felt like I was in another world. In a way I was, mentally and emotionally.

When we are in such times, the enemy of our souls, the devil, is quick to take advantage while we are in a weakened state. I was doing things I needed and enjoyed—praying, going to church, painting, listening to upbeat praise music and hymns, spending time with caring friends, reading the Bible, and listening to encouraging messages on Christian radio. All these things were excellent; but depression continued to hover over my joy. The worst of it was I felt like I couldn't hear God. He seemed so far away.

I felt spiritually numb. It was awful. It lasted a very long time, even while I continued to read the Bible, pray, and journal about my experiences. It was puzzling and very disconcerting to feel removed from my usual optimistic nature. I was functional, and even went to work,

69

but I was miserable and my emotions were unpredictable. Because I had always worked to keep my emotions under control, it was disconcerting to have tears suddenly well up, or an unexplainable sense of panic that would compel me to suddenly leave a perfectly normal and enjoyable social gathering.

If you are in a fragile emotional state, please realize you are not alone. Others of us have been, there, too. And God brought us through, just like He is going to bring you through and you will be fine again. You are not unique in your struggles. There is hope, even if you can't feel it right now. God's Word reminds us He is the help for the helpless, our provider and sustainer. Not only is He mighty God; He is our gentle Shepherd. There are things we don't understand about what happens in our lives or why, but God never wastes any of our experiences, even those that seem pointless or counter-productive to us. God knows what to do with them to shape our lives. It has been said that our trials will last only as long as they are needed for God to lovingly accomplish in us what He has planned for us, for our good and His glory.

I told a dear friend about my difficulty in shaking off the darkness. She was a nurse, and recommended that I see a doctor. I really wasn't sure about going to a doctor about it. But it was good advice. The diagnosis was situational depression. This is temporary depression that arises from specific events that heavily impact and disrupt the normal chemistry that keeps a body in emotional balance. I was grieving four deaths and the aftershocks of a deceitful relationship. My doctor gave me a prescription and it helped a lot. After a few months, my body chemistry became stabilized, and I no longer needed the prescription. The doctor guided me as I reduced the dosage and after a few more weeks I was done with it.

The dark cloud had lifted enough to let a little sunshine in. I began to think more clearly. But I still didn't feel completely back to normal. Providentially, my sister-in-law invited me to attend a women's Christian retreat with her at Cannon Beach, Oregon. It is a location I love, but I hesitated. I wondered if I could function normally in the group gatherings without those strange sudden panic feelings. I didn't want to have to deal with trying to explain to someone how I was feeling, because I didn't really understand it myself. I hesitantly accepted her invitation, hoping I wasn't getting myself into a situation where I would feel "trapped" so far from home.

At the retreat, I met a Christian counselor who spent an hour with me, listening, praying, and talking with me in a healing conversation that broke through the wall of deception that had been holding me captive. I saw it was more than my emotions at work against me. It was a demonic oppression that could only be broken by spiritual means, the work of God. Identifying the enemy and addressing the true source of the bondage I was feeling was key to my complete release from those lingering dark feelings. As the counselor guided me through scriptures (many of which are in this book) and prayed over me and with me, an unexpected attack occurred. It was a strange experience. As I began to pray in the authority of Jesus' name, a sudden horrendous headache thundered in my head. It was so intense that it alarmed me, and I raised my eyes questioningly, telling the counselor what was happening. She calmly asked me, "Can you keep praying?" I nodded, and she said, "Then keep going." By the time I was finished with my prayer, the headache had receded, and I felt emotionally released. A sense of freedom flooded into my soul. In discussing the experience with her, I recognized that a tremendous spiritual battle had taken place. The crazy headache was a physical signal of the intensity of the battle. I believe it was the devil's attempt to distract me from the one authority, Jesus, who could release me from the enemy's grip. The enemy had to bow to the name of Jesus. That was the focus of the prayer, and that was what happened.

This was a dramatic event. I have not had any like it since then. I believe it was an experience Christ wanted me to have to impress upon me the reality and strength of spiritual warfare.

It became a pivotal point in my faith, to understand how real the spiritual realm is and how actively it surrounds and influences us. We do not need to fear it, because God has given us His power and guidance to combat evil. But we do need to be keenly aware of it, so that we know how to address obstinate situations that confront us.

Not all depression is from a spiritual source. And not all depression is from a physical or psychological source. Sometimes it is a combination. We need help to identify the sources so that we know how to face it and overcome it. In my depression, it wasn't from a single source. It originated from a combination of grieving, chemical imbalance, and spiritual battling. God used several people to completely deliver me from that unshakable depression—my friend's urging to see a doctor, my sister-in-law's invitation, the doctor's prescription, and the

Christian counselor's wise spiritual discernment. The final stroke against the enemy was the supernatural deliverance of God's power and grace exercised on my behalf. All were God's provision to deliver me out of the pit, and how I praise Him for it. He is our faithful deliverer.

It is amazing to me how the Lord released me from that emotional quicksand. God so often works in surprising ways, ways we never imagine. At the Christian retreat meetings, it wasn't the primary retreat speakers God used to help me. They were good. But God used a secondary party to help me. God brought me to the location where He had a counselor who was prepared to discern my need. She had followed the leading of the Holy Spirit to volunteer to meet with anyone who might need to talk. It wasn't the usual format of the conference to have a counselor available and volunteering her services. I didn't know when I talked with her what would come of it. But God knew. The counselor knew how to win the battle against the enemy. I didn't. I needed her. This is another example of how wonderfully God works on behalf of His children when we don't even know the right questions to ask! Ephesians 3:20 says God "is able to do exceedingly abundantly above all that we ask or think, according to the power that is at work in us." That power that works within us is the power of the Holy Spirit, of course.

1 John 4:5 tells us, "For this purpose the Son of Man appeared, that he might destroy the works of the devil." God demonstrates His power to triumph over the devil as He did at the cross. He also does it in our daily lives. Jesus is still all about destroying the works of the devil. Jesus is the strong protector of His own, that gentle Shepherd, but also the Mighty Most High King of kings and Lord of

lords! Do not think you are outside the love and power of Christ. God has taken great care to make sure we have the information we need to survive the battles we face in this life. He has given us His Word for our instruction and for our encouragement. We receive power as we read in His Word, believe it, and act on it.

THE SWORD

I was talking to a friend the other day, and she told me about her sword. Not a physical sword. She was talking about the sword of truth and power that Jesus Christ has equipped us with for spiritual battles on this earth.

"For the weapons of our warfare are not by our flesh and blood, but are mighty through God to the pulling down of strongholds, casting down imaginations, and every high thing that exalts itself against the knowledge of God, and bringing into captivity every thought to the obedience of Christ." (2 Corinthians 10:4)

I notice that our weapons are mighty through *God.* It is He who casts down the enemy. It is He who pulls down strongholds. The arena is the realm of our thoughts and imaginations. The power of God reaches into every thought that is opposed to the truth and knowledge of God. Our weapons bring every enemy into captivity. That is power! That is victory!

We need to be constantly aware of this marvelous power that God has conferred upon us. And we need to access it, not just know it is available "in case we need it someday." We need it every day. Like Mary said to me regarding the mental battle she was facing, "We need to sharpen our swords for what we are facing in life." What a true picture!

How do we keep our swords sharp? We sharpen our swords by reading the truth God has recorded for us in the Bible. Then we know what's going on around us, and what provision God has made for us—not just to survive, but to thrive in this world—to have victory over emotional downers. We cannot avoid experiencing emotions, because God created us as emotional beings. But we do not have to become victims of our emotions. Let's sharpen our swords!

As we talked, Mary said, "My sword has been dragging. I haven't been carrying it. I've been letting it just drag behind me. I need to regather strength and hold my sword high!" I agree. It's great that we own a sword, but unless we use it to defeat the enemy, it is of little effect. Just holding up a sword in the face of an enemy and saying, "See my sword?" isn't going to do the job. We have to wield it in battle, use it. What does that look and sound like?

The sword of the Spirit is the Word of God. (Ephesians 6:17) You read the Word. You land on a scripture that speaks to your need and you meditate on it. Let it sink in. Consider how it applies to your current situation. You write it on a post-it note and put it where you are reminded of it often. You memorize it. (Don't say you can't memorize. You can. It requires full attention and plenty of repetition. You can do it. God wants you to carry it with you at all times. God will help you.) You speak it out loud to solidify the words and to put the enemy on notice that you know the truth and will not succumb to his lies. Then you act on the truth of the Word. This is what seals it in your mind and spirit. It becomes part of your experience, not just head knowledge. This is how you sharpen our sword for its mighty work. The enemy cannot stand against God's truth.

There are physical causes of depression that should be ruled out. When there are physical causes for depression, overcoming discouragement and depression is sometimes won with medical help for a chemical imbalance in the brain or body. I thank God for the medical help that is now available for such cases. Fortunately, the stigma attached to depression is going by the wayside as medical science explains the changes that occur in the brain and body, indicating real conditions that can be measured. No more "Just buck up, get over it, quit feeling sorry for yourself."

When there are spiritual causes for depression, victory over discouragement and depression must be won through spiritual avenues. The Bible is clear about the spiritual battles Christians face. The Bible is also clear about its instructions for us for victory. It is up to us to take the instructions seriously and follow them, whether we understand them or not. That is the exercise of faith. "And this is the victory that overcomes the world, even our faith." (1 John 5:4)

We don't always know which causes are foremost, so we pray for insight, and take each avenue we have to reach the answer. There are answers and remedies. Ask for help if you are suffering and are not able to pull yourself out of it with your best efforts. We are not meant to go it alone. God means for us to get the help we need.

In my case, there were combined sources of my depression. Grieving the losses of my loved ones who died, and the deception I fell prey to afterward, caused my self-confidence to plummet and revealed ugly spiritual pride that the Lord needed to wash out of me. In the process, I whimpered to Mary, "I feel like grapes in a winepress and I'm being stomped on over and over." Her cheerful response was, "Well, let's pray that God gets good juices from it." No pity party participant was she! It was not particularly comforting, but it was very insightful. Good juices did eventually flow from the stomping! Stomping bruises and growing pains are not fun, but they can lead us to a place we need to be—pliable and humble and tenderhearted in new ways. And that's all good.

During my time in the winepress, I felt so very alone. I was single, with family living many miles away. I was a widow after 29 years in a wonderful marriage. I began to write down my thoughts, feelings, and insights that I received as I read the Bible and prayed. It helped a lot to write it out. It helped me sort through all the churning, confusing things I was feeling and experiencing. Very often as I wrote, my journaling session became a prayer time and I wrote out prayers, too, as my thoughts flowed. I wanted to have a record of what I was feeling and how God would speak to me in my heart and mind and answer my prayers. Those records encourage me today when I read how God showed me He was at my side. I still journal during times when I am wrestling with peculiar events, things I don't understand and don't know how to react to. It helps.

JOURNALING
I urge you to consider journaling as you work through

discouragement and depression or any other trial. It takes time to write, and that is an advantage when dealing with hard experiences! It slows us down long enough to more thoroughly process the events that are troubling us. I think it also slows us down enough that we can hear what God is saying to us. You will be surprised what you learn while you are journaling. Journaling is a valuable tool for gaining insight about yourself and others, and it's comforting to be able to release emotions on paper where you can privately vent, cry, rant and rave, and not create turmoil for those around you! Some of that journaling I have now thrown away, after working through some excruciating things that would only hurt someone to read them. That is a very wonderful thing about journaling. You can holler, scream, complain and whine on paper, then throw it all away without hurting anyone in the process.

The psalms that David wrote are wonderful examples of how the Lord works to move our thoughts away from ourselves and our problems and redirect them towards His power, glory, love and faithfulness. So many of the psalms begin with a description of David's troubles, but end with his praise to God. Turning our thoughts to the Problem-solver certainly helps. A phrase David used was, "So I encouraged myself in the Lord." David had no one else around him to encourage him. So he encouraged himself! It is a good reminder for us. Remember God's faithful intervention and help from former times. Read God's principles and promises in His Word. Tell yourself the Truth! It is both instructive and encouraging.

Just the other day, I was reading the Old Testament account of Jacob wrestling with a man who is commonly interpreted to have been an angel. I thought, That is what

I was doing during my winepress time! I was wrestling. Like Jacob, I was pleading, "Lord let me hear from You! Bless me! I won't let go of you until I hear You!" If you're familiar with the story of Jacob, you remember that as he wrestled, his opponent touched Jacob's thigh, putting his hip out of joint. Jacob continued to hang tough, even with his hip out of joint, and insisted, "I will not let you go unless you bless me." And the angel blessed him, saying to Jacob, "Your name shall no longer be Jacob, but Israel; for you have striven with God and with men and have prevailed." (Genesis 32:24-30)

What does this story have to do with discouragement and depression? It's an example God gives us to learn from. The parts of this story that strike me are:

• Jacob was alone before the wrestling match began. Sometimes we need to feel our aloneness, our helplessness, before we are ready to receive a blessing from God.

• Jacob persevered because he desperately felt his neediness. He needed a blessing.

• Jacob was given a hindrance in the process. His hip went out of joint. But he didn't let the hindrance deter him from his focus—to receive God's blessing.

• He wrestled with God, insisting he would not quit until he received a blessing.

• He received the blessing! He received the blessing! Got that? He received the blessing. His persistence paid off!

God is not reluctant to bless us, but our self-will is very strong. My self-will wants to prevail, and I don't always recognize it as unproductive willfulness. So God interacts with me in such a way that causes me to finally recognize through the struggle and wrestling, that all I want—bottom line—is God Himself, His comfort, His strength, His love. When we are in a place of darkness and difficulty, we become keenly aware of our need for God. It brings us to a point of giving up on ourselves, our resources, and those things we keep in mind that we can always fall back on if everything else fails. In the winepress, I felt perplexed, confused, and disillusioned. "I want to hear from you, God!! Why can't I hear you?!" was my cry. I was wrestling with God. Not against Him, but with Him. The wrestling was my cry to God: "Let me know you are with me! Bless me! I need you! I will not let You go until You bless me!"

I had discovered my own resources were not enough. It was a deeper realization of my need than I had had previously, and a humbling experience. And the Lord did bless me! He brought me relief in His timing. There are more details of my release from depression that would take a few more pages to describe. They were both dramatic and instructive. The whole experience enriched my appreciation of how beautiful and perfect, powerful, and personal, God is; and how tenderly He was watching over me the whole time, during the time when I thought I couldn't hear Him! This fortifies me for today's difficulties.

Looking back on that time, I clearly see examples of His protection over me while I floundered and struggled. Yes, He was there all the time. Sometimes our struggles are so severe that we can't see Him or feel His presence at the time. It is not because He isn't there. It is because of our overwhelming emotions that blind our spiritual eyes and desensitize our awareness of His presence and His love. Other times, with an overwhelming barrage of emotions, some may deliberately push God to the back burner. But He doesn't go away.

God is all about relationship with His children. He allows trials in our lives to help us recognize our need for Him. They cause us to want to draw closer to Him. Our stories will be different, but His ultimate purpose is consistent—to build and strengthen our relationship with Him. He will exert His power over the enemy in this world and will show His love and faithfulness to His children.

If you are wrestling with God, it is certain that God has a special blessing prepared for you. In the wrestling time or the waiting time, here are God's Words of encouragement to you, His precious child:

"Draw near to God and He will draw near to you." (James 4:8)
"Lo, I am with you, even to the end of the world." (Matthew 28:20)

In Jesus' name, and for His glory and honor, I offer these words as an example for you to speak out loud to the enemy, as is, or in your own words:

Right now, I use this, my sword of Truth as the authority to declare that In the name of Jesus, I am now taking authority over every source of evil influence that attempts to exalt itself in my mind and emotions against the knowledge of God. I give them no room for any negative effect on me, for I belong to Jesus who has all authority. This is all spoken in the authority that Christ Jesus has given me as His child, and as His servant of the Most High God. All things are always under the authority of the name of Jesus. It is written "for this purpose the Son of God came, to destroy the works of the devil." You devil and demons have no power over me. I declare that I believe God's Word and that Christ always leads me in triumph. I believe His Word that says, "Thanks be to God who always leads us in triumph in Christ, and through us diffuses the fragrance of His knowledge in every place. For we are unto God a sweet savor of Christ…" I take that truth and declare that it is operational in me, right now, by the power of the Holy Spirit. You, demonic forces, were defeated at the cross. I am saved by the shed blood of Jesus. You have no place in my life and I give you no place. Get out in Jesus' name!

Now, I pray to God:

Thank you, Lord, for Your wise and loving purposes You have for me that You are working out even now. I believe Your Word. I trust You. You know my heart. Please bless me with a growing relationship with You. Strengthen me against all the attacks of the enemy. Thank You for fighting these battles for me in the power of Your Holy Spirit. All praise and glory to You! In the strong and mighty name of Jesus! Amen.

When we are fighting spiritual battles, we do it in the name of the One who conquered death and the devil. We speak God's Word. Open your Bible and read it out loud to the enemy if you don't have it in your memory. We declare truth to the enemy. You speak it into your environment, knowing that the invisible spiritual realm is alive and present, filled with both angels and demons. It is different from prayer. Prayer is directed to God. Prayer is our conversation, confession, adoration, and supplication to God. The Holy Spirit leads us in both actions—declarations and prayers—and accomplishes His purposes in all our statements of faith.

QUESTIONS:

1. When are you most susceptible to discouragement and depression? Tired? Hungry? Lonely? Angry? Around certain people? After certain input like nightly news, reading material, TV, or movies?

2. Who do you know who will listen and give you godly input when you are discouraged and depressed, without promoting a pity party?

3. What encouraging scripture has helped you redirect your thoughts and encouraged your faith when negativism tries to gain supreme attention of your brain and emotions?

4. How can you sharpen your Sword this week? What will help you persevere?

5. What are you willing to do the next time discouragement hits you and you feel yourself sinking into the quicksand of depression?

STEPS:

1. Be aware of your thoughts. "Think on things that are true, pure, lovely, of good report. If there be any virtue, if there be any praise, think on these things." Phil. 4:8

2. Avoid negative input. Books, news, movies, television, negative people that feed into your discouragement and depression will work against you.

3. Write out your thoughts in a journal. Take time to consider truth.

4. Write down ways you remember God has answered prayers and provided for you and is still providing for you. (Encourage yourself, like David did.)

5. Get medical help and counsel, if needed. Don't go it alone.

6. Speak the truth of God's Word aloud. Quote Scripture. Often. As often as needed until the negative thoughts are replaced.

7. Pray. Let God hear all your thoughts. Listen to what He impresses upon you. Write it down!

8. Let others pray with you and for you.

PERTINENT SCRIPTURES:

Jacob wrestles with the angel.   Genesis 32:24-30

"When I am weak, then am I strong." 2 Cor. 12:9-10

He "is able to do exceedingly abundantly above all that we ask or think, according to the power that is at work in us." Ephesians 3:20

"Now thanks be to God who always leads us in triumph in Christ, and through us diffuses the fragrance of His knowledge in every place. For we are unto God a sweet fragrance." 2 Corinthians 2:14

"David was greatly distressed…but David encouraged himself in the Lord his God." 1 Samuel 30:6

"…the Sword of the Spirit is the Word of God." Ephesians 6:17

"Above all, taking the shield of faith, with which you shall be able to quench all the fiery darts of the wicked." Ephesians 6:16

"Think on things that are true, whatever is honest, just, pure, lovely, of good report. If there be any virtue, if there be any praise, think on these things." Philippians 4:8

7 Fear and Anxiety

Don't we each have a lion to face from time to time? I know we do because the Bible tells us, "Be sober, be vigilant, for your adversary, the devil, walks about like a roaring lion, seeking whom he may devour." Not just a lion. A roaring lion. A hungry lion. Scary, indeed!

We are warned about the lion—not to scare us, but to prepare us. It is worth taking note that the lion is only seeking whom he may devour. He's seeking, he's looking around. Maybe he'll find someone. Maybe not. It's not a sure thing! He may devour. Or… he may not.

It is up to us whether the lion gets a meal out of us, or not.

When someone says, "fear and anxiety," what comes to your mind? Probably as many different ideas as there are people reading this book! We each bring our own set of experiences, backgrounds, and emotions with us, and they are shaped differently in the same way our fingerprints distinguish us from one another. But the overall experience of fear is common to us all.

Some fears are healthy. They keep us away from dangerous objects and situations. These fears have been learned, and wisdom is the result. If certain environments or circumstances have proven repeatedly to be dangerous or potentially dangerous, it is wise to pay attention and not place ourselves in places where bad things have happened previously. These are healthy fears that help us make wise decisions about any involvement.

But many fears are not healthy. Unhealthy fears are made up of imagined "what if's," potential scenarios, insecurities, and unknowns we rehearse in the darkened theaters of our minds. They are issues we have no control over, and no reason to believe they will actually happen. Nevertheless, we worry our fear will become reality. This becomes an issue of faith and is something we can control.

The big question is, how deep are you willing to go into God's grace and promises of protection, provision, and victory? You know and I know from our experiences that God is our Champion, and He leads us through the most unexpected paths to grow our faith and to bring us ever closer to His heart. Unhealthy fear is from the enemy. Every fear of uncertainty, doubt, worry, anxiety is from the enemy. When fear is from God, we know in our spirit that there is a real danger, not just a worry, anxiety, maybe-the-worst-will-happen or what-if feeling! God will convict us of danger, real danger, in an unmistakable way, when we need it. He is our Shepherd, and will call us by name, and no other voice will we choose to follow! So, it's helpful to know which voice we are listening to at any given moment. That is my prayer for you, that you will recognize the voice of the Shepherd, and follow that voice. You will. I have no doubt. That you will recognize the voice of the thief trying to get into the sheepfold, and you will turn a deaf ear; that it will be mumbo-jumbo in your hearing.

"For God is not the author of confusion, but of peace." (1 Corinthians 14:33)
and
"For God has not given us a spirit of fear, but of power, and of love, and of a sound mind." (2 Timothy 1:7)

It's always imperative that we remember the character of that prowling "lion." Jesus called the devil "the father of lies." "He does not stand in the truth. And there is no truth in him," Jesus said. Unhealthy fears are based on lies that come to our minds or that others sometimes suggest to us. How important for us to realize that fears are based on things that haven't happened yet! We suppose they may happen. We imagine the worst that could happen. We fear what will happen. But we don't really know what will happen. It is all in our imagination and hasn't played out yet.

We are assured of victory and restoration because we choose to refuse! We refuse to fall prey to the devil's schemes. "Resist the devil and he will flee from you," the half-brother of Jesus writes. (James 4:7) We will don our armor and wield the spiritual weapons God has equipped us with. We need to do battle.

89

One of the insidious aspects of fear is the way it affects our bodies. When our mind thinks of fearful things, it activates the body to prepare for "fight" or "flight." Adrenalin begins to increase, and heart palpitations occur. The body doesn't know the difference between what our minds are imagining, or if we are actually experiencing the threat we are rehearsing in our minds. This is not a good thing. It means our bodies and emotions are going through the stress of an experience as if it is really happening, right now. Who needs extra stress? It is one very good reason to avoid entertaining fears and imagining the worst that might happen. Don't rehearse such scenarios in your mind.

As in other emotional battles, we must first become aware of what is confronting us. Once we realize how fear acts and the damage it causes, we are motivated to give it no tolerance, and to practice overcoming it. Practice is effective in the physical realm. It is also effective in the emotional, spiritual, and mental realm. There is a practical way to put fear in its place—and that place is in a corner, a very small corner. The method is surprisingly simple, and very effective.

Think about this for a moment. Fear and trust are exact opposites. We cannot fear and trust at the same time. It's impossible. Here is an easy exercise to prove we really can't consciously concentrate on two different things at once. Let me ask you to spell your name right now. Now, count backwards from 20, right now. Either one of those instructions is easy to carry out. But now, spell your name in your mind, and at the same time count out loud while you are spelling your name in your mind. Can't do it, can you? We have to let go of one thought to concentrate on the other, no matter which one we try to do out loud. This seems like a silly exercise until we realize this is a powerful truth that we can put to work to rid our minds of fearful thoughts and unhealthy thinking patterns. Deliberately focusing on positive thoughts leaves no room for the negative, fearful thoughts. It takes practice, and you can do it.

It is not Pollyanna thinking. It is a rational choice to let go of a worrying frame of mind, and renew our thinking with God-given truth. Now that we realize we cannot fear and trust at the same time, it becomes a choice about which attitude to focus on. Fear? Or trust?

Fear seems to come more naturally to us. It's the path of least resistance. However, it's not the best way to spend our mental and emotional energy. I was listening to a presentation by a noted neuroscientist, Dr. Tim Jennings. He spoke about scientific research that has been done recently on the brain, concerning the effect of faith and positive thoughts about God's love. The study found measurable chemistry changes in the brain to compare.

Dr. Jennings said, "What we *believe*," he said, "holds power over us, *physically*." This is something to pay attention to! Neuroscience validates this, using brain imaging and measurements. Studies show improved physical responses in heart rate, blood pressure, and other experiences when the brain consciously focuses on the positive messages of God's love. Believing in a God of love calms the body and mind. Lies disrupt our thinking and cause adrenal reactions. If it goes on for years, our brain circuitry changes and becomes like a snowball rolling downhill. Dr. Jennings explained in the study that it gets worse with practice. We actually lose healthy circuitry. There is a connection between the brain and spirituality. The brain circuits reacting to fear can become overdeveloped by over-exercising them. This is both a warning and an explanation for those who are already haunted by fears. Habitual thinking patterns affect us—for good or for evil.

Satan works tirelessly on believers to try to get us to believe wrong things about God and about ourselves. The effect of wrong beliefs causes anxiety, fears, hopelessness, and even physical problems. There are many erroneous beliefs being bandied about by unbelievers. There also are false impressions and completely wrong thinking about God that even some Christians hold onto. They bring their painful experiences and past misunderstandings into their theology, and ask questions like, "If God is a God of love, why would He allow that to happen?" They draw the wrong conclusion that God must not be all that loving, after all. And therefore if He is not loving, He cannot be trusted.

Bingo. Satan has scored a hit and disabled faith through confusion and lies. This is not the fault of the believer. Satan is a relentless enemy and he doesn't play fair. He preys upon the weakened, the injured, the ill, and the distressed. Just like a lion after its prey. However, even though it is a constant battle, there is good news. We may be the devil's prey, but we are not helpless.

As in other emotional battles, we must be aware, first, of what is confronting us. Once we realize how fear acts upon us, and the damage it causes, we are motivated to give it zero tolerance, and to practice overcoming it. As we mentioned, practice is effective in the physical realm, for athletes, musicians, chefs, etc. It is also effective in the spiritual realm. Practice creates habits that become a part of us that we can bring forth when needed. It helps produce successful responses to unexpected events or requests when we have practiced and created good habits.

This works just as well in times of emotional and spiritual challenges. We have developed habits of thinking and emotions that have not been helpful to us. These have, in fact, created problems. So how do we correct wrong thinking patterns that have become so ingrained they are a natural part of our instant reactions to things? There is a practical way to put fear back in its place. The method is surprisingly simple, and very effective.

Are you ready for a short lesson on neuroplasticity? You can impress your family and friends when they ask you what you are reading these days. "Oh, I read about neuroscience and neuroplasticity!" you may say, and you'll be telling the truth! Here it is:

Neuroplasticity is a good thing. Neuroplasticity refers to the flexibility of our brains. New patterns in the brain can be created. Negative brain patterns can be healed even after being established by years of negative thinking. Remember what Dr. Jennings said. "Fear circuitry can become overdeveloped by over-exercising it." The best part is the opposite is also true. Studies show that the brain's circuitry can be re-routed for healthy connections and freedom from negative thinking.

A certain brain research study used subjects who were 65 years and older, to study brain patterns that had been well-established over a lifetime. One group of subjects was given the assignment to meditate 12 minutes a day on God in the context of His love. When compared to the other group of 65-year old persons who did not meditate on the positive attributes of God, the meditating group showed measurable positive changes in the brain. In addition to the changes in the brain, there were also physical changes, too. Improvements! Improved heart rate, lowered blood pressure. Just from meditating on truths about God's love 12 minutes a day every day.

This answers the question, "How do we correct our wrong thinking patterns that have become habitual and ingrained?" It is a spiritual discipline. We do it consciously. It doesn't come automatically. If it were an unhealthy eating pattern, I would have to restructure my thinking, deliberately. It doesn't work for me to just agree I have an unhealthy eating habit while indulging in a plate of fudge brownies or a bag of potato chips every day. I can't just acknowledge it and then wait for it to correct itself. In order to be healthy, I have to deliberately choose to teach myself about what I'm eating, and then work to change it to better serve my body. It is a decision.

In a similar way, to restructure my brain circuitry takes a commitment from me, a serious decision. It won't happen by simply wishing my way out of fear and anxiety. Just as I have to make a decision and a meal plan to restructure my eating habits, I need to make a plan to restructure my wrong thinking, recognizing that I need God's help to be successful. I am counting on His power to come alongside my decision to follow-through.

With that, here is what works:

1. Remember, remember, remember that Satan is the father of lies.

2. Remember you have the source of all Truth. Truth is revealed in the Bible. God cannot lie. (Titus 1:2)

3. Think about Jesus, Immanuel, God with us, who was the walking embodiment of God in the flesh showing us God loves, protects, provides, counsels, delivers, heals, seeks tender hearts, and heals the hurting.

4. Spend time getting to know God's heart. Read His Word. Perfect love casts out fear. Faith comes by hearing, and hearing by the Word of God. (Romans 10:17)

5. Read the gospel of John and soak in the many words of God's love for you.

6. Pray. Take time to be still in body, soul, and mind, and know that God is on your side. Ask for His help.

These truths will begin to wire themselves into your brain circuitry as you purposely focus on them. Steps you take will have this rewiring as their foundation. You can begin today and immerse yourself in it. What is needed is a strong foundation to build the steps on. Don't neglect the foundation. You may have to unlearn some wrong thoughts. Focusing on the truth will correct those. Your subsequent steps are listed at the end of this chapter.

I am not denying there are things in this life that are powerful triggers to set off fear. As we said earlier, some are based on past experiences that hang with us and are difficult to shake. Sometimes we need help in order to ward off fear. I want to tell you about a time when I encountered a powerful attack on my mind and emotions. It was beyond my ability to manage on my own, even as I struggled to exercise faith to overcome the pronounced fear—it was probably what is referred to as a panic attack, at least something like it. It required help from my praying friends.

In 2008, my husband was in the living room, exercising with his usual routine. I was in another room, working in my office. From my workroom, I heard what sounded like snoring. But it was very, very loud, much more so than normal. I thought he had fallen asleep, but after a minute, I felt compelled to check on him because the snoring sound didn't sound quite right. When I saw him lying on the floor, I realized that something was very, very wrong. Without warning, his heart had stopped beating. It's called Sudden Cardiac Arrest. I rushed to his side and saw he was unconscious. His color was gray. He had no pulse and he wasn't breathing, except for reflexive gasps of air that were occurring. They were the sounds I thought were odd snoring sounds. These, I learned later, were agonal gasps, a sign of imminent death. Tom didn't regain consciousness from the CPR I gave, nor from the EMT's who came when I called 911. He lay in a coma in the Critical Care Unit on life support. It was a fearful time.

He was in the hospital, in death's grip, and his organs ceased functioning, one by one. On the third day, God gave him an amazing return to life, restoring his failed organs, one by one. There is much more to the story, which I wrote about in *Faith Refined—Holding on When Life is Falling Apart,* because that's what I was doing, just holding on. It was a miraculous work of God that restored life to Tom. His return home after three weeks in the hospital was cause for amazement and rejoicing.

But our minds and emotions work in peculiar and unexpected ways at times. The major crisis was past, but when Tom came home from the hospital was when I had the panic attack. He was in an extremely weakened state when he was sent home from the hospital. I was terrified of him coming home because of his physical weakness and my inability to physically support him to help him get around the house. I recognized the physical challenge. What I didn't expect, though, was the mental and emotional trauma I would experience.

The first night that Tom was home, I awoke next to him in bed. He was snoring loudly. It brought back with traumatic vividness the moment that I had found him on the floor of our living room. Hearing his snoring, I consciously knew that Tom was alright, because this time he was breathing. But I couldn't suppress the terror I felt at the sound. I was experiencing PTSD—Post Traumatic Stress Disorder. I wanted to scream. I wanted to run. I don't think I even thought to try to get him to roll over. I didn't want to disturb him. He needed to sleep. But I was in a total panic. With my heart thundering, I went into the living room and stuffed a pillow against my face to muffle my sobbing and to suppress my intense desire to scream. I felt out of control in an overwhelming way.

Here is my point:

Although my brain was telling me the correct facts— Tom is alright. He's home. He's breathing—my emotions were shouting, hollering, screaming at me, "It's just like what I heard when I found Tom three weeks ago!" I tried desperately to reason my way out of the terror of the moment, but I couldn't make my emotions behave by simply talking to my brain, trying to talk sense to myself. This was clearly a kick from the enemy while I was down.

I was consumed with irrational fear. And nothing I thought or tried helped me gain control. It was a dreadful night.

I prayed all night, willing with all my might to be rid of the terror, without success. God knew all about it. In His love, He caused a praying friend to call me the next morning and ask if she and another friend could pray with me. YES, oh, YES! I was so glad to be offered such a gift. I knew I couldn't make it through another night like the one I had just experienced. My best efforts had not been enough to help myself, and wouldn't be enough; I didn't want to have to even try to make them enough!

I needed to be free to talk about my terror without distressing Tom, but I feared leaving Tom alone. He assured me he would be fine for the time I would be gone. I met that morning with my two friends, who counseled me with the Word of God, reminding me that God had already worked a miracle, reminding me that God doesn't "toy with our emotions," reminding me that the enemy, the devil, was taking advantage, trying to undo the glorious amazement and praise to God we all had experienced, knowing the miracle God had worked. Reminding me that we needed to take authority over the devil's schemes and the attacks of fear and panic he had caused the night before. They read to me some selected psalms about God's power and love triumphing over all our enemies. One was Psalms 34:4. "I cried unto the Lord, and He heard me, and delivered me from all my fears."

Our prayer time was focused on God's goodness, His power, His glory, and the defeat of the enemy at the cross through the shedding of the blood of God's only Son,

Jesus Christ, Messiah, Almighty God, King of kings and Lord of lords. As we prayed, I cried and cried, releasing the physical, emotional, and mental tension that had been weighing heavily on me during the trying days in the hospital while Tom lay in a coma, and then the difficult days following. As we concluded our prayers, I felt the burden lift. I felt faith return in full force with wonderful freedom in my spirit. The battle with the fearful lion—the roaring lion—had been won. The battle for faith was victoriously finished. God always wins.

Yes, God always wins. Please remember this. God always wins. Whether fear or anxiety over large or small things, God always wins. When we rely on Him, He wins the victory for us.

God has given us provisions for times of unfair attacks. We are fortunate, so blessed, to have our protective equipment and supplies close at hand, if we will just use them. If we believe correctly, we have healing working in our brains, working to bring back stability and correct thinking, delivering us from our fears.

We have steps to take. Sometimes, like the paralytic with his four friends carrying him to Jesus, we need our friends to carry us. My two friends took the initiative and offered to carry my burden when they asked if they could pray for me. Are we willing to help carry each other? We must be! This is God's beautiful plan—that we do not have to go into battle alone. He has given us one another for burden bearing and battling.

As we have seen, there are two kinds of burdens referred to in a surprising pairing in Bible. In Galatians 6:2,

Paul writes, "Bear ye one another's burdens, and so fulfill the law of Christ." What is the law of Christ? It is the law of LOVE.

The burden referring to a heavy, unmanageable burden—like a large boulder—was the burden of irrational fear that I desperately needed help to bear. How wonderful of God to work in the hearts of my friends to call me and offer their love, their listening ears, their calm and steady counsel, and their prayers. I was too distraught to have thought of calling anyone. It didn't occur to me. I pray that I will be as sensitive to the nudging of the Holy Spirit as my friends were to me that morning. They heard from the Holy Spirit and responded with love and action.

Jesus Christ carried the ultimate burden, taking what we could not bear on our own. He took the punishment that we deserve for all our sinfulness, willful disobedience, and folly. This is the kind of burden-bearing the God of Love has done for us. He is our Burden Bearer, carrying the boulder of sin that was our burden—and we accepted His gift of burden-bearing. With that gift came His forgiveness through the shedding of His blood for the remission of sins, the forgiveness of our sin. We are called to care for one another, to bear burdens in prayer and in counsel, and in practical ways of helping one another, and so fulfill the law of Christ. What is the law of Christ? The law of Christ is LOVE.

Why did Jesus come? 1 John 3:8 gives a wonderful reassurance for every battle we face against the roaring lions in our lives. "For the Son of God appeared for this purpose, to destroy the works of the devil." We are able to be free of the devil's work in our minds, emotions, and anything he attempts to dislodge or destroy in our faith. Jesus came to destroy the works of the devil. This is truth.

Years ago, I was taking an outdoor painting class. My two children were with me, playing nearby. The location was a picturesque woodland stream. It was a beautiful day. We were accustomed to spending time outdoors in similar surroundings, and the kids enjoyed playing on the shallow stream's edge and tossing pebbles into the water. I looked up from my watercolor paper and was horrified to see my adventurous seven-year-old son had climbed onto a tall structure that stretched over the water. He was up high, on the swaying partial remains of what probably had been a wooden bridge. There wasn't much left of it.

Seeing the dangerous swaying, I gasped and ran towards Brian, calling out instructions to him to wait. He was moving backwards in the direction that he had climbed, like one does when you descend a ladder. I could hear him talking to himself, muttering, and he wasn't paying any attention to me. He was making very slow progress. My heart was pounding, and I wondered how in the world I could help him. The structure swayed menacingly, and I was sure that if it swayed under his little body, it certainly wouldn't be steady for me.

I stood under him, thinking I could break his fall if he lost his grip or if the section were to give way, which seemed imminent. Brian was still talking to himself, but I couldn't hear what he was saying. At last he made it to the ground. After hugging him with a pounding heart and great relief, I asked, "Why were you talking to yourself? What were you saying?" He looked at me with his serious brown eyes and said, "I was saying, 'I will trust and not be afraid. I will trust and not be afraid. I will trust and not be afraid.'" It was a Bible verse he had learned a few days earlier in a Good News Club. Out of the mouths of babes, right? What a good example to follow!

We are assured of victory and restoration because we choose to refuse! We refuse to fall prey to the devil's schemes. "Resist the devil and he will flee from you." We will don our armor and wield the spiritual weapons God has equipped us with. We are more than conquerors. Read all of Romans, chapter 8. It is so rich and reassuring of God's love for you.

"For whatever is born of God overcomes the world. This is the victory that overcomes the world—our faith!" (1 John 5:4)

"Behold, God is my salvation, I will trust and not be afraid; For the Lord God is my strength and song, And He has become my salvation." (Isaiah 12:2)

These are all words of truth to speak aloud to silence the devil's temptations to fear and be anxious. Resist him with God's truth and trusting statements. Satan cannot stand against truth. He hates it. And you win.

If you are not accustomed to speaking out loud against spiritual forces, it will seem a little odd to you at first. I assure you, however, that godly men and women for centuries have exercised this authority and testify to its effectiveness. The spirit world is real. We have to overcome our ignorance or lack of awareness of its existence, and face it boldly with the weapons Christ has given us to maintain victory by faith.

We walk by faith and not by sight. We cannot see the invisible world, but the Bible speaks of it clearly and instructs us to be vigilant, be bold, and be full of faith through the power of the Holy Spirit. The authority of the name of Jesus is awesome and undefeatable. "The name that is above every name" is Jesus. Every being, earthly or spiritual, is under the authority of the name of Jesus, and we speak in the authority of His name, "in the exceeding greatness of His power." It is the name of Jesus that causes every knee to bow.

"Therefore God also has highly exalted Him and given Him the name which is above every name, that at the name of Jesus every knee should bow, of those in heaven, and of those on earth, and of those under the earth, and that every tongue should confess that Jesus Christ is Lord, to the glory of God the Father." (Philippians. 2:9-11)

And
" …that you may know what is the exceeding greatness of His power toward us who believe… far above all principality and power and might and dominion, and every name that is named, not only in this age but also in that which is to come." (Ephesians 1:19-21)

Notice the repetitive theme about faith and overcoming the world and the wicked one in 1 John. The word is written to tell us the truth about who we really are. We are overcomers!

"Because you are strong, and the word of God abides in you, And you have overcome the wicked one." (1 John 2:14)

"You are of God, little children, and have overcome them, because He who is in you is greater than he who is in the world." (1 John 4:4)

"For whatever is born of God overcomes the world. And this is the victory that has overcome the world—our faith." (1 John 5:4)

"Who is he who overcomes the world, but he who believes that Jesus is the Son of God?" (1 John 5:5)

QUESTIONS:

1. What areas of fear or anxiety seem to get the best of you?

2. How will you resist the devil the next time you are faced with fear or anxiety?

3. Find a scripture that addresses your fear. Write it down. Post it on a mirror or somewhere you will see it often.

4. What does the Bible say about your situation? About you? Let others help you find one or more scriptures that will be truths you will cling to and declare when you are faced with the enemy's threats and lies. Write them here:

STEPS:

1. Choose to win over fear. This is a spiritual discipline and God helps us with it. The Holy Spirit "works in you both to will and to do God's good pleasure," Phil 2:13 says. "Submit yourselves to God. Resist the devil and he will flee from you. Draw near to God and He will draw near to you." (James 4:7-8)   But you must choose.

2. Remember that fear is built upon lies, and lies come from the devil, the father of lies. Like a house of cards, recognize them, and force them to crumble under your resolve to choose truth and to speak truth.

3. Remind the devil he was defeated eternally at the cross. His attempts to undo what Jesus accomplished are futile. Jesus Christ came to destroy the works of the devil and you belong to Christ. You will believe the Word of God and will not agree with lies and worrisome speculations that are suggested to your mind by anyone, anything, or in any way.

4. Choose truth. Remember you cannot think two opposite things at the same time. You cannot think about truth and lies at the same time. Choose to reflect on the truth.

5. Choose everything you think about. Think about God's promises and trust Him. Choose trust! "I will trust and not be afraid," Psalms 56:11 says. Say it out loud.

6. Speak the truth out loud as often as necessary until the lies subside. Be persistent. Don't give up. The

105

enemy will test your resolve to defeat him. Believe God's Word and announce it. It isn't positive thinking. It's truth. It is your battle sword!

7. Pray, and have others pray with you to defeat fear and to be reminded of truth.

PERTINENT SCRIPTURES:

"The Lord is my light and salvation, whom shall I fear? The Lord is the strength of my life—of whom shall I be afraid?" Psalms 27:1

"Do not give place to the devil." Ephesians 4:27

"Resist the devil and he will flee from you." James 4:7

"I cried unto the Lord and He heard me, and delivered me from all my fears." Psalms 34:4

"Behold, God is my salvation, I will trust and not be afraid; For the Lord God is my strength and song, And He has become my salvation." Isaiah 12:2

"I will trust and not be afraid." Psalms 56:11

"Submit yourselves to God. Resist the devil and he will flee from you... Draw near to God and He will draw near to you. " James 4:7-8

"For the Son of God appeared for this purpose, to destroy the works of the devil." 1 John 3:8

"Don't be anxious about anything, but in everything by prayer and supplication with thanksgiving, let your requests be made known to God, and the peace of God which surpasses understanding will guard your hearts and minds through Christ Jesus." Philippians 4:6,7

"For God gave us a spirit not of fear but of power and love and self-control." 2 Timothy 1:7

Read all of Romans, Chapter 8. You will be blessed and will probably see a scripture that is "just for you." Write it below.

8   Inadequacy and Insignificance

We have been thinking about living with a different mindset, experiencing victory over negative thinking and emotional reactions that blindside and sideline us before we know it. We've thought about the deep meaning of victory according to God's perspective, in an eternal context, empowered by the Holy Spirit and secured in our inner being.

We've thought and prayed about achieving lasting and satisfying freedom by applying truth in the face of common stresses like hyper-responsibility, fear and anxiety, discouragement, depression, false guilt, and unjust accusations.

All these emotions, if they are not confronted and remedied, play into creating feelings of inadequacy and insignificance that sometimes get the better of us. We've realized that in order to see things properly we need to get our perspective from God instead of from other voices and influences. How wonderful that God has given us His very words to instruct us, and His Holy Spirit to live within us to help us do just that.

The fruit of the Spirit is love, joy, peace, long-suffering, goodness, gentleness, faith, meekness and self-control. When I notice I'm missing any of this, I know that I've lost God's perspective; and I need to take time to reorient my thoughts and my attitude God-ward. The fruit of the Spirit in action supplies us many proofs that we are *not* powerless or inadequate.

We have known or read about individuals who are facing great adversity who still are able to exhibit fresh faith and are upbeat and joyful while suffering. We admire them and realize they are living at a level that is supernatural. It gets our attention because it is in stark contrast to the responses we commonly see and feel. Even though our natural tendency is to respond with the same level of emotions we are attacked with, we can choose to respond in the Spirit.

Inner peace in the face of antagonistic and combative people is a great victory. The enemy will use others to accuse, whisper insinuating lies, or treat us with contempt and indignity. Sometimes it comes from strangers, sometimes from co-workers, sometimes even from family members. Some experiences are so daily and repetitive they can skew our perspective of ourselves over time. But we don't have to live with the skewed perspective. It can be reversed, and it should be. You and I, dear friends, are greatly loved by God. He considers us worth dying for! How remarkable is that!

With this topic, inadequacy, I cannot help but be impressed with the amazing statement of the apostle Paul when he said, "Most gladly, therefore, I glory in my weakness, for when I am weak, then I am strong, for the power of Christ rests upon me." Of all people to say he ever felt weakness, I least expected Paul to say it. He had asked God to remove a thorn in his flesh, and God told him, "My grace is sufficient for you." (2 Corinthians 12:10) God was pleased to allow Paul to experience His strength that He would give him in place of Paul's human weakness. Paul's response to that was to glory in the answer, trusting God to take over and fill in the gaps! We do the same.

I have been incredulous when people have told me, "You are very strong," when I knew in my heart and body that I felt as wobbly as if I were walking a window ledge on a skyscraper in an ice storm. One of those times was during the grieving and suffering I wrote about earlier. I could not have felt less strong. Yet, God was holding me in His hand, holding me up, and His strength was apparently showing during my weakness. This is quite a wonderful thing to realize. When we feel inadequate, it is a terrific opportunity for God to work. He will work as we trust His truth, and move forward with the expectation

111

and faith that He will do what He says—make His strength complete in us while we feel most weak. Don't worry if you feel weak. Feeling weak forces us into a humble attitude. It isn't comfortable, but it is good, because "God resists the proud but gives grace to the humble." (1 Peter 5:5) His grace is what I need. So if weakness makes me humble, good! Then I am in a place to receive God's grace.

God, our Creator, gives us our true self-worth and significance. If we are going to live in truth, we must soak in God's words about us. Past experiences can trip us up from accumulated words that demeaned us. A lack of appreciation, thanklessness, and words left unsaid can do almost as much damage as outright verbal attacks. Here again we must realize the sources of our wrong feelings about ourselves. Exposing the source is the key to averting a sneak attack.

A sense of inadequacy or insignificance may have begun in childhood from actions and words directed at us by other children or adults. Young children have not developed a filter for what they say or hear, and those hurtful words can stick. It really isn't true that "sticks and stones may break my bones, but words can never hurt me." Words can do a lot of damage. They hang in the air and ring in our ears. When we are children, we have not developed the maturity to be able to judge what's true and worthy of consideration, against what comes from a temporary explosion of uncontrolled anger or frustration, or other reasons for words that are spoken against us. As children, we simply hear it and accept it as truth, not knowing any better. Ill treatment from childhood falls into the same category. Deliberate blows were not deserved. It is how they are interpreted by the young mind that creates lasting damage. The bruises have long since healed, but inner brokenness still remains. Jesus came to heal the wounded and the broken-hearted.

A sense of inadequacy or insignificance may have begun in adolescence. The teenage years are a minefield of ugly remarks and rude occurrences that can affect lives into adulthood. I can still remember remarks that were made to me when I was in seventh grade! How ridiculous to allow those remarks to shape my sense of self-worth. They were made by immature rude youths. My adult friends tell similar stories of unforgotten words and injuries from that time of life. Why do we give them any thought or credibility now that we are adults?

Since being an adult, I have met and have had to deal with a few "adolescents" in grown up bodies. Their feet got bigger, but their emotions did not keep up with their feet. They still respond in immature, unacceptable ways. The world will always have bad-tempered under-developed persons. I am sorry for them, but I do not have to feel forever wounded by their inappropriate and thoughtless remarks. I admit that it takes conscious effort to ward off my initial instantaneous negative reactions and desire to "hit back." But that's exactly the point. It takes conscious effort. That is what we are doing right now as we think through each scenario, each source.

Receiving others' assessments of you into yourself as if it is Truth—as if it is the last word regarding your worth—is a big, big mistake. A celebrity wisely said, no matter what words are said about him, he takes them with a grain of salt. He said he is neither as wondrously marvelous nor as desperately despicable as anyone may say. That is likely true of all of us, and a good attitude to assume.

What really counts is Christ's assessment of us. To gain correct perspective on ourselves, we should make time to think about what God says about us. What great worth you have, as God's beautiful creation! He says you are worth dying for. As one who has received Christ's salvation, you have been given all things that pertain to life and godliness, with a multitude of promises from God. To read a full description of this, drink in the words from 2 Peter 1:3. Drink slowly. It is exceedingly rich. Savor and digest each phrase.

"Grace and peace be multiplied unto you through the knowledge of God and of Jesus, our Lord,

According as his divine power has given unto us all things that pertain unto life and godliness, through the knowledge of him that has called us to glory and virtue;

By which are given unto us exceedingly great and precious promises, that by these you might be partakers of the divine nature, having escaped the corruption that is in the world..."

As we have already considered, we can pray for strength to take persecutions or insults against us (whether spoken out loud or harbored in a thinly veiled way) as Christ did. We are called to "endure it patiently, for this is acceptable to God" when we suffer for doing good. We can waste much energy and lose much sleep trying to defend ourselves against unfavorable circumstances and vengeful adversaries (family, coworkers, even strangers with road rage). Thinking "I should have said this," or "I could have done that," or planning future follow-up actions for the next time such a thing happens or is exhausting. It drains our energy and emotions. Worse, it drains our ability to experience and enjoy God's love for us, which is a constant faithful presence in our lives.

Realizing and receiving the truth of God's love is the key to living with freedom every day. Focusing on what God thinks and living with the knowledge that He is on our side reorients our perspective on everything. His calling to us is that we be partakers of His divine nature. His divine nature. That is amazing. I can hardly wrap my mind around it. He allows us to live life with a conscience that is free of guilt; for we know when we sin, we can confess it and be restored to intimate fellowship with God immediately. He forgives us.

Realizing God's love creates an eagerness to love Him back. Focusing on God's love gives us confidence that when we fail, we can be forgiven. When we doubt, He will counsel us. When we are weak, He will show Himself strong on our behalf. If you need help grasping the truth of these statements, give yourself an assignment to read the gospel of John, and take your time with the reading, soaking in the words of Jesus as He spoke about Himself and His heart's purpose for coming into the world for you. For you! It is stunning truth. It will refresh you, inspire you, and greatly comfort you.

Christ won a great victory for us, not just for our future heavenly home, but for our earthly now existence, too. Victory is won in specific ways, but it is more than a specific event. It actually is a universe of overcoming power. It is our entire environment, a new atmosphere, because we are connected to the Almighty God, King of kings, and Lord of lords, the one who is always victorious. "Now thanks be to God who always causes us to triumph in Christ." (2 Corinthians 2:14) God means for us to dwell with awareness of our overcoming environment, to transform from our human nature into that divine nature, changing as we gain knowledge of all that He has provided for us, and all that He is for us every day. He deserves our loyalty, devotion, and obedience. I want to love Him more. My prayer is, "Lord I love you. Help me to love you more! Help me to be acutely aware that You are with me everywhere I go."

Joseph in Genesis is an example. Joseph was a young man of integrity whose older brothers hated him and sold him into Egyptian slavery. Things went from bad to worse for Joseph in Egypt. He was falsely accused and thrown into prison. It's quite the story with a wonderful turn of events. God's plan for Joseph was fulfilled in Egypt. Joseph forgave his brothers and later said to them, "You meant it for evil, but God meant it for good." Sometimes God removes us from family interactions for our blessing or protection-- spiritual, emotional, physical, or otherwise.

The awareness of God's presence must have been what kept Joseph going strong when he was betrayed by his brothers, sold into slavery, and ended up in prison. Twice in Genesis 39 it records, "the Lord was with Joseph." A reminder that even when it isn't readily apparent, or easily discerned, the Lord is with you because you matter to Him. I pray He will make this so real to you that you will recognize it with great joy. When we really KNOW this truth and begin to live with the awareness of it, it renovates our life. We let go of attitudes and habits and compromises that have held us back from a life of freedom and joy. We embrace the changes, believing what is written in Jeremiah 29:11, "God has plans for you, plans for your good, to prosper you and not to harm you. Plans to give you a hope and a future."

This truth is good for every season of our lives. When I became a widow at age 49, it rocked me. I felt disoriented and unsure of what the rest of my life would look like. God clearly gave me some desperately needed reassurance in a totally unexpected way. I was finishing the school year of teaching 4th grade, struggling to cope with the loss of my husband, wondering where my life was headed now that my beloved husband was no longer with me. I had not expected him to leave this earth at such a young age. But it did not catch God by surprise. In fact, He had planned a surprise to encourage and comfort me through a pizza event, of all things. Three teachers, including me, with three classes of 4th graders numbering 90 students altogether, were at the end-of-year event at a local pizza parlor.

In the midst of the gooey, cheesy pepperoni pizza feast, a student called out to me, "Mrs. Donivan! Mrs. Donivan! What does this mean?" His outstretched arm was waving a flimsy paper napkin at me, which he had pulled from the café-type napkin dispenser on his table. Puzzled, I came to his side, and saw that words were written on the napkin, in handwriting that appeared to be a young teen's. I was bowled over at what I read, and asked my student where he found the napkin. He showed me that it had been carefully folded and layered with other paper napkins in the dispenser. The napkin apparently had been intended to be discovered at some unappointed time by an unappointed pizza customer. When I saw the words, I knew it was not a haphazard appointment. The neat, rounded hand lettering on the napkin displayed, "He who began a good work in you will carry it on to completion until the day of Christ Jesus. " (Philippians 1:6)

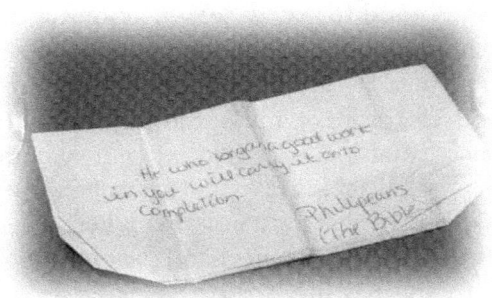

It was meant for me, I was absolutely sure. I was stunned. I so needed that! It was a lovely reassurance to me that God knew where I was, what I was going through, and wanted me to know His plans for me were not thwarted or detoured. He was completely in control and leading me as always, even though the circumstances in my life had changed drastically. When I recovered from my astonishment, I asked my student if I could keep the napkin he had pulled from the dispenser.

Over 20 years later, it is a treasure I still have. It reminds me of the innumerable ways and remarkable timing God uses to comfort and speak to His children in need. Each day, He knows my need, my heart's cry. Planning well beforehand, He has already provided His answer for me, for the moment it will mean the most. Our Father wants nothing more than for His children to experience His encompassing love in ways we won't forget.

No wonder I still have that paper napkin! And that scripture will always be a precious one to me, reminding me of His nearness and caring, that of all the napkins in all the dispensers in that restaurant, He arranged for me to be the one to see that particular napkin at such a time. Don't overlook these kinds of events, or brush them off as coincidences. God speaks to you, specifically you. We are not in a spacious auditorium hearing His voice. He speaks to each individual according to his or her need. He whispers it in your ear and makes sure it is a way you will understand, because He longs for you to know His voice.

God has delightful, unexpected ways to speak to us, doesn't He? He knows which kinds of things will impact us, catch our attention, and reveal His love in the most meaningful way to fit our individual personalities. Oh, rejoice and revel in those special moments! That moment when a Bible verse just exactly fits what you need. It is a love gift from God, just for you! A word of encouragement from a friend, affirming you, just when you need it.! A beautiful display of His handiwork in a rainbow, flower, or a sunset to show you His power and glory, fortifying your faith, just when you need it. Another love gift from God, just for you!

Whether others are impressed with the event doesn't matter. When it impresses *your* heart, you know that God sees you, and like we read in Genesis, "the Lord was with Joseph." God wants you to know He is with you, just as surely. Put your name in the phrase, instead of Joseph's. The scripture says, "And the Lord was with Joseph." And then, "But the Lord was with Joseph." Say, "And the Lord was with _____" (Put your name in here). Now, because there is a different sense to beginning that sentence with the word "But", say it again, putting your name in the sentence, "But the Lord was with _____." Say it out loud. This is truth. There is power in speaking the truth to yourself out loud. You hear it as you speak it, and so does the spiritual realm. It is reinforcing.

God has plans for you, individual you, just as He does for me. His plans for me have often been very unexpected and have evolved from season to season. I am in the latter season of life now, and different changes have caused me to readjust in a number of areas. Physically, I cannot do many things I love to do.

While I was wishing and working toward certain things, God was quietly working on other things for me that I had no idea of. Somehow, God led me from teaching elementary school to beginning an online business teaching watercolor painting, which led to writing and illustrating a children's book, which led to other books, and then to beginning a second business, publishing books. I never dreamed of such things! But God did. Somehow He gets us where He wants us to be. I often think, "Yes, He accomplishes what is needed in spite of my flailing and floundering." I don't know how He does it, but He does. I am always astonished.

I'm reminded of a humorous statement I heard many years ago, about an "Eleventh Commandment." Oh, you didn't you know there is an "Eleventh commandment?" It is, "Thou shalt not sweat it." It makes me smile. We "shall not sweat it," because God is the one who is at work in us "to will and to do His good pleasure." We need not worry because He is trustworthy. We cannot see the future, but

God can, and He gets us where we need to be. It will be the place that is a fit for the season of life we are in. That's His plan and that's how He works.

Are you single? God has a plan and special things for you in your season of independent decision-making and freedom of choice. You have many options, and God is faithful to guide you in the ones that will bring blessing to others. And you will also be blessed, in the process!

Are you a parent of young children? Talk about making a difference and lasting effects! Your current assignment is eternally significant. You may have dreams of what you imagine are grander things to do, but God is using you to shape your special children for eternity through your interaction with them! Your love and provision for those precious ones has an effect on their development and talents that no one else can influence the way you can.

Are you a parent of teens? That is a job! Talk about the need for flexibility, perseverance, patience, and wisdom. I learned a lot about prayer when my children were little, but I learned even more about the power of prayer when they were teens. These are stretching times, but, like Joseph, "the Lord is with you" in the challenges. Sometimes it appears as if everything we do to raise our kids has no effect on them, and we can feel as if all our efforts are worthless. Don't worry. It's only temporary. God is on your side, and He is impressing your children with more truth than you realize.

Are you at retirement age? It has a new set of challenges, doesn't it? If we've left a job that gave us

121

satisfaction and a sense of purpose, it is common to wonder at some point if we have any value, any worth, now that we are out of the work force. Or what to do now that we are away from daily family interactions with children and their activities. Our earlier sense of meaning can feel foggy, and we wonder, "Okay, what now?"

Single life and family life each have a mixture of pain and pleasure. All of life is a huge growing time for exercising faith with changing seasons. Seasons of pressure and seasons of relief. Through it all, God wants you to know how valuable you are to Him. You are not insignificant. You are not inadequate. You can do all things through Christ who strengthens you and leads you in triumph. The more you read the Bible, the more you will see it and believe it. The Bible is more than a guidebook for living. It is powerful and empowering Truth. It transforms our thinking and our emotions as we drink it in and dwell in it (contemplate, pray, and enjoy it).

Above all, God loves you with an everlasting, never-failing love. It is constant every day, on your good days and on your bad days. You are precious to Him. Sometimes I think we spend too much time studying the Bible, and not enough time enjoying the Bible, reading the love letters God has written to us, eager to see what He will say to me today, to encourage me and remind me that He shows Himself strong on behalf of those who love Him. Think of those times when He has done this for you. Revel in it. Let Him love you!

Jesus Christ personified victorious living in the face of all kinds of stresses. Daily pressures from confused disciples who didn't understand, and crowds of people clamoring for his attention, his help, and his healing power. Direct conflict from those who opposed Him. False accusations, and efforts to trip him up with contrived questions and manipulations. And finally, the most vicious effort of all, to do away with Him and His followers through betrayal and crucifixion. Little did Jesus' adversaries know—the cross was not a defeat for Christ. It was His great, glorious victory for all time! It didn't catch Him by surprise. From the beginning of time, it was His plan to triumph over evil forever, knowing we, His beloved created ones, would need His salvation.

What looked like a defeat in the eyes of His enemies was actually the grand, victorious crescendo in God's symphony of love through Jesus' life on earth in the flesh. At the cross, in His final hours on earth, Jesus took upon His own body the excruciating and ultimate punishment sin deserves. Not for His own sins, for He was without sin. But for our sins. As He suffered and died, He gave the greatest gift of all to all of us—forgiveness for our sins forever, paying the ultimate price, suffering and dying— taking our place for the punishment we deserve.

In case His disciples missed it, Jesus told them clearly, "No one has greater love [nor stronger commitment] than to lay down his own life for his friends." (John 15:13) What other friend do you have who would give up his life for you? How remarkable, to think that our Creator God loves us so much that He prepared a way for us to live with Him forever in a forgiven state, with no reminders of our evil ways, our failures, our mess-ups. The Bible tells us, "As far as the east is from the west, so far has He removed our transgressions from us." (Psalms 103:12) Through His death, God's Son proclaimed His love, essentially saying,

"I accept your punishment, I accept death, to pay the complete penalty for your sin; I accept your punishment for you, so that you can be free of condemnation and judgment, if you will only accept the gift of my life—the penalty having been paid on your behalf." And miracle of miracles, through His resurrection Christ proved He has power over all things—sin, death, and life eternal!

Now Christ has conferred upon us power to do all things through Him. The Bible says we are more than conquerors through Him who loved us! We are seated with Him at the right hand of God, a position we have through Christ's death for us and His resurrected life. He reigns, and we reign with Him! The Bible tells us these amazing facts. Let its immense significance sink in.

Let us remember that sometimes what looks like a defeat in our lives is actually a path to greater victory, personal victory. God's ultimate plan often includes surprises, and His surprising work in our lives is the one that counts! Watch for God's sweet indications that He is with you. He knows we need His reassurances. Cling to them. Encourage yourself in the Lord by remembering times of refreshing that He has given you, and His unique surprising messages which appear on paper napkins, or from a phone call, or some small thing that means so much at exactly the time you need it! And especially, read and remember His promises in the Bible.

Just to listen and be listened to is a beautiful gift in a day. Find a prayer partner if you don't have one. It is a gigantic blessing to have someone to call and pray with over the phone, or to get together with for prayer and encouragement from the Word of God. Get God's perspective! That's how we do it. We won't have it if we don't expose ourselves to His truth. Make time for Him every day. Expect Him to speak to you through His Word. He will. That's why He gave it to us! This isn't an assignment that you have to feel guilty about when you forget to do it, or miss it for one reason or another. It's not an obligation. It's a beautifully wrapped gift from God that He offers you. Take advantage of it. Open it up.

Victory has been won and given freely to us by Christ Jesus. Our part is to receive it thankfully. It takes a conscious effort and mental discipline to not give in to the path of least resistance. Make a conscious choice to overcome. Jesus' last days with His disciples were a time of earnest teaching, telling them to remember the significance of His love for them, His sacrifice, and His triumph over death and sin, freely given. Jesus said to His disciples, "Remember. Do this in remembrance of me." Remember His love for you. You are ever so precious to Him. If that is hard for you to accept, tell Him so. Ask Him to open your eyes and your heart to His love. He will do it. He wants you to know you are His beloved.

His life, His death and resurrection demonstrated His sacrificial and immeasurable love and valuation of you and me—indescribable gifts to us of love, life, and victory. He gives it to us—both for our here and now, and for all eternity. That is undeniable evidence of your value and significance. Take His Word for it!

QUESTIONS:

1. What childhood or adolescent messages still ring in your ears?

125

2. What voices, now or in your past, most influence you regarding your sense of self-worth?

3. Who or what have you been listening to that you need to ignore in order to correct a wrong sense of inadequacy or insignificance?

4. What weakness (inadequacy) will you give God for Him to show His strength through you?

5. What truth from God's Word speaks to you to correct your thinking about inadequacy or insignificance? (Write it down and memorize it! Speak it aloud!)

STEPS:

1. Read the gospel of John, focusing on the love Jesus displays. It all applies to you.

2. Be glad when you feel inadequate. It is your opportunity to watch God show His strength in your weakness!

3. Accept that life is full of various seasons. The Lord is with you no matter what season you are in. Repeat "And the Lord was with _____" (your name)

4. Ask God to show you what about your character and what you are doing that He values. He will do this. Write it down to record what is true and good.

5. Reflect on this often: God values your life above His own! He gave His Son's life to save yours.

6. Repeat what God's Word says you are: Say, "I am... His precious treasure, His child, His friend, His chosen, His beloved, a royal priesthood, a joint heir with Christ, the dwelling place of His Holy Spirit."

7. Accept unavoidable changes that require adjustments in your tasks or focus. God is working to show His strength in and through you. God is for you. God is with you. (Joseph's story, Genesis 37-45)

8. Enjoy the rests and refreshment God gives you between seasons of change. It is part of His preparation and plan for you. God is always working to prepare you for now and also for your next season.

9. Believe God's Word first and supremely for your sense of worth and true significance. Don't trust your emotions which are subject to change. God's Word stands firm and never changes. Trust Him to bring about every blessing He has planned for you. God cannot fail.

10. Pray. Ask God to replace erroneous impressions you have of yourself with His truth. Thank Him for His great love for you and the great value He has placed upon your life with Him.

11. Listen for His reassurances. Write them down.

12. Think about others. How can you encourage someone today?

127

PERTINENT SCRIPTURES:

"That is why, for Christ's sake, I delight in weaknesses, in insults, in hardships, in persecutions, in difficulties. For when I am weak, then I am strong."
2 Corinthians 12:10 NIV

"Behold what manner of love the Father has bestowed upon us, that we should be called the children of God." 1 John 3:1

"By this we perceive the love of God, because He laid down His life for us." 1 John 3: 16

"We love Him, because He first loved us." 1 John 4: 19

"For whatever is born of God overcomes the world; and this is the victory that overcomes the world, even our faith." 1 John 5:4

"God works in you both to will and to do His good pleasure." Philippians 2:13

"Grace and peace be multiplied unto you through the knowledge of God and of Jesus, our Lord, According as his divine power has given unto us all things that pertain unto life and godliness," 2 Peter 1:2-4

"I can do all things through Christ who strengthens me." Philippians 4:13

"And God is able to make all grace [every favor and earthly blessing] come in abundance to you, so that you may always [under all circumstances, regardless of the need] have complete sufficiency in everything [being completely self-sufficient in Him], and have an abundance for every good work and act of charity." 2 Corinthians 9:8 AMP

OTHER SCRIPTURES ABOUT YOUR SIGNIFICANCE:

■■■

YOU ARE

In the household of God, a fellow citizen with the saints -- Ephesians 2:19

chosen, royal, holy -- 1 Peter 2:9

joint heir with Christ -- Romans 8:17

child of God -- Galatians 3:26

Jesus' friend -- John 15:15

chosen, without blame -- Ephesians 1: 4, 5

more than conquerors -- Romans 8:37

God's workmanship -- Ephesians 2:6, 10

■■■

9 Hopelessness

Hopelessness, for a Christian, is an embarrassing admission. We, of all people, are meant to be people of hope. The gift of salvation brings with it the promises of God recorded in the Bible; they are the undergirding of our faith. We have felt the joy of God-fulfilled promises. We have seen and heard of miraculous interventions for safety, healing, provision, inner peace. We have even had our own wonderful experiences that have proven that God is the God of hope.

Yet, in any of our lives, we are subject to losses, some of which are so devastating we wonder how we can go on. We are threatened with loss of expectation, loss of faith, loss of hope. Hopelessness may encroach upon our sense of well-being through losses like death, betrayal, illness, natural catastrophes, financial crisis, or other traumas. Sometimes we feel as if we were singled out by some capricious, unfair ruling of the universe. The hurdles look insurmountable. We feel helpless and hopeless. When struggles become ours—not just events we read or hear about in others—malicious attacks are launched against our thinking, emotions, and faith.

Most of us have experienced at least one event that caused us to fall into a chasm of hopelessness. I certainly have. One of those times stands out as a dramatic example in my mind. It was a day that felt like a tectonic shift under my feet.

I had been experiencing months of increasing physical difficulties, and had been puzzling over why my efforts in the swimming pool and with fitness equipment had not yielded any benefit. Then, a defining incident occurred in my garden, of all places. I spotted an irresistible glacier-blue hydrangea bloom for a summer bouquet. Leaning a few too many degrees beyond vertical in my effort to clip it, I executed an ungainly Olympic tumble into the center of the shrub.

Mortified, I instinctively craned my neck to see if anyone had witnessed my spectacular landing on the hydrangeas. Realizing how Hollywood-esque it was struck me funny. But then I realized I wasn't going to be able to get to my feet again, and there was no one to call for help. I felt like a giant walrus draped on the landscape, clumsy and comical.

With Herculean effort and a great deal of walrus huffing and puffing, I bodysurfed through the sea of hydrangeas and crawled to the front door. The drama seemed deserving of applause. But it was also a moment of Truth. I finally had to acknowledge something was badly out of order with my balance and coordination; I anxiously waited for a doctor's appointment.

Then came the doctor's somber pronouncement, "You have adult-onset muscular dystrophy. It is a progressive disease, it will get worse, and there is no cure." This explained the weakening leg muscles and wobbly balance I had been doggedly fighting for some time without success. My mind and emotions silently screamed, "NOOOOOO!" Protesting would not make it better. I couldn't fix it. I longed for a giant "Reset" button that would restore me to earlier days when I was projecting a very different plan for my life.

I couldn't contain the tears; they came in a tsunami. However, I recognized my greatest enemy wasn't the disease. My greatest enemy was a sense of hopelessness. Its evil suggestions echoed back and forth, flinging taunts of resignation and defeat:

"It's never going to get any easier."

"You don't know how long you will be able to perform daily routines."

"You don't know how long you will be able to stay in your home."

"You don't know the rate at which your abilities will fade away."

"You won't be able to travel to those people and places you want to see."

"You won't be able to…" etc., etc., etc.

There were so many unanswerable questions about my future. I was sure of one thing, though. I didn't want my dismay to paralyze me and define me. Giving in to the twin feelings of helplessness and hopelessness is like succumbing to ravenous monsters in the dark. They hover and taunt, wreaking havoc on our abilities to plan, to create, and to enjoy. No wonder God tells us over 100 times in His Word, "Fear not!" He knows how many battles we will face in this life, what makes us tremble, and how prone we are to just give up. So, with His clarion call to "Fear not!" He assures us He will be with us. How many times have I worried and stewed, only to see things work out just fine after a while, sometimes without any action or intervention from me!

It wasn't easy to "wait, and give it some time" instead of letting panic take over. But with all the determination I could muster, I held panic's flailing elbows and fists at bay. I applied the Three Day Rule. I had tested that theory before, and found it is often true, right on schedule. So, I waited and prayed.

"Wait on the Lord. Be of good courage and He will strengthen your heart. Wait, I say, on the Lord." (Psalms 27:14) I see that we are to be of good *courage*. It takes courage to wait, especially when we feel weak, worn, and hopeless. It takes time for enemies to be summoned out of the shadows and become exposed in the light of objective truth. Psalms 36:9 declares, "For with You is the fountain of life. In Your light we see light." David, the psalmist, had many dark experiences that he wrote about. He was clear about where his courage came from. "You, Lord, keep my lamp burning; my God turns my darkness into light." (NIV)

134

Knowing David could face armies and saboteurs day and night and yet find hope and strength from God encouraged me to march forward to face my sense of hopelessness. My march forward would be for a confrontation not only to survive, but to thrive. My aim was to rob the darkness of its frightening ogres, and find whatever blessing might be waiting in the dark for me. Many things we fight and flail against are actually God's mysterious ways to draw us into His embrace and reveal His love and power to us. Even Joshua needed to be reminded by the Lord to be strong and courageous.

"Be strong and of good courage. Do not be afraid, nor be dismayed, for the LORD your God is with you wherever you go." (Joshua 1:9)

I made a conscious mental shift away from the black clouds gathering in my imagination. I substituted a mental picture of a cleansing rain shower pouring from those same threatening clouds, washing away anger, fear, bitterness, and hopeless negativism. Free of the junk, I knew I would be able to think more clearly, consider the options, and develop a plan.

Exposing the enemy, hopelessness over a life of weakening muscles that I can do nothing to prevent, meant I must be boldly realistic. I needed to accept what I can no longer do, and then focus on what I still can do, making the most of things that are fulfilling and motivating for me, and taking one day at a time.

"Forgetting the things that are behind...I press toward the mark of the high calling of God in Christ Jesus." (Philippians 3: 13-14)

135

Like Joshua, I must remember "for the Lord God is with me wherever I go." When I am out of answers for myself, and know only God can make the difference, I am in a place designed for blessing. Giving myself this pep talk, I prayed for God's comfort, guidance, and strength and, most of all, His help for helpless me.

After three days I sat down with paper and pencil. And I took stock. Reality: I was a classroom teacher, and I had loved it, but my stamina could no longer hold up for classroom teaching. Nevertheless, I still felt a fervent desire to be an encouragement to others and give tools for enjoyment and success in their personal lives. How could I do this now? To identify what I had to work with, I decided to make a list:

What Still Is

- I enjoy sharing knowledge to help others.
- I like to encourage others to become the best they can be.
- I am creative with art and video.
- I love color.
- I love painting. People ask me to teach them how to paint.
- I enjoy writing.
- I like learning new things.

With my list before me, I pondered how I could put some of these attributes together logically and use them in new ways in spite of an unpredictable disease. As in most other first-time journeys, I took a brave first step with no assurance that it would become anything significant. But it led to the next step, then the next. Looking back, I can see Jesus' "footsteps in the sand" at each point in the process.

The first positive step came when I noticed that now I would have time to paint again; I hadn't had sufficient time to paint while I was teaching. I knew I couldn't stand in front of a classroom any longer; but I could teach beginning watercolor techniques through video demonstrations. So I took it on. Onlookers would have laughed hilariously to see me filming my art lessons. Even though I had previously demonstrated the same painting techniques numerous times with students, now face to face with the unblinking video camera lens, I produced enough bloopers and dead air to inflate the Goodyear blimp!

Finally, many weeks and bloopers later, the videos were edited and completed and became part of a beginning watercolor painting kit. This, my first project, evolved into an online business, teaching beginning watercolor techniques. It was fun to create, and has been fun to hear how others enjoy using their simple watercolor materials to create greeting cards and paintings for relaxation and art therapy.

Unexpectedly, that led to a second project—writing a children's storybook about color mixing, which I illustrated with fun-loving toucans. Creating it was an exhilarating seven-month excursion. Between story writing sessions I painted and cut out paper characters, then photographed them on watercolor backgrounds for the illustrations. I felt like I was back in the classroom, laughing with my second-grade students, snipping scissors and splashing paints. Creative activities, whether they produce professional-looking or amateur-like results, are therapeutic. Art therapy and music therapy are effective for all kinds of emotional and physical needs and are now used extensively for patients in healing environments and homes. An unexpected bonus was that it was also uplifting for me to create materials which I believed would be fun for others.

When I completed the toucan book, I faced the inevitable challenge all authors face—getting it published! I investigated different publishing options and attended Writers and Illustrators conventions and Publishing conferences to learn the professional aspects of publishing. That led to starting a small company to publish uplifting and entertaining books. I am meeting wonderful authors, and am feeling fulfilled while working with them to get their books published.

Each of these projects required new skills, and have kept me busy for weeks, months, and years. Each venture has been work, but a lot of fun while learning new things. New projects fuel my imagination for the next opportunity that might be waiting in the wings. Creativity generates optimism and hope. "Call to Me and I will answer you and show you great and unsearchable things which you do not know." (Jeremiah 33:3 NIV) Very often, the first creative effort will lead to another one. It gets those right brain (the creative side) juices flowing.

I began to wonder about children who have muscular dystrophy and others who are wheelchair-bound from an early age. I wondered if they had sufficient guidance and encouragement to develop their abilities. Do they realize how much happiness they can bring to others through their special talents and interests? Do they experience joy in their own lives, realizing their great value, even though they may not be able to do all the things their friends and other children do, free of disabilities?

I tried to find entertaining children's books geared toward this subject, and there weren't many. I wanted to add to the category and encourage these children. For the next six months I wrote and illustrated a picture storybook about Kevin, a young boy in a wheelchair, who discovers abilities he doesn't know he has. *Wings for Kevin* is meant to do more than entertain with bright colors and a flying unicorn. It's meant to inspire children to "find their wings" like Kevin does.

But such aspirations are not only for children. You have skills, talents, and interests that can be expressed in many ways. Some may be dreams of yours that have not yet been explored. Others may be found in new hobbies, or through suggestions from friends or family, or chance happenings that pique your imagination. Even bad tidings can become the impetus, just as muscular dystrophy and negative feelings that threatened my peace of mind nudged me toward new experiences. Taking on new projects gave me a happy distraction, hoping the projects would produce something for another person to enjoy.

Doing something for another person is a rejuvenating experience. It reminds us we have traits that other people enjoy and need. In the mire of hopeless feelings, we may not remember such things. In spite of your feelings, try to pay attention to what others are saying to you, particularly about what you have done or can do. Consider these things as possible endeavors now. Giving our attention to the needs of others helps reduce our own downcast feelings, and goes a long way to creating a new sense of purpose in the place of hopelessness. I began doing things I had not given any thought to before the physical decline of my body. These new explorations have given me fresh perspective and fun projects. It's true that I miss certain things that I can no longer do, and I have to resist temptations (and there are many) to dwell on the losses. Instead, I try to let my imagination and God's inspiration lead me toward new adventures that He knew I would need during this time of my life. What He has prepared me for He will see me through.

"For we are His workmanship, (His own master work, a work of art), created in Christ Jesus for good works, which God prepared for us beforehand (taking paths which He set), so that we would walk in them (living the good life which He prearranged and made ready for us.)" (Ephesians 2:10 AMP)

If I am His workmanship, then God still has work for me, right now, even if it does not go in the direction or have the appearance that I expected. Jesus said, "I have come that you might have life and have it more abundantly." Okay, so this wasn't what I thought of for abundant life. But if God thought of it, and is working it out, I want to get on board!

It's so important to keep an open mind when wild winds are whirling and storms are thundering around our paths. In spite of my weakening body, the "real me," the "me" inside, is enjoying showers of refreshing rain that God faithfully sends with the dark days of dwindling physical abilities. Whether the enemy is illness, loss,

140

disappointment, betrayal—or any other potentially disabling circumstance—taking time, summoning the enemy out of the shadows, and allowing God's light to shine on it all invites a new array of possibilities. I am seeing it work out. Long ago, God knew about the gene in my body for adult-onset muscular dystrophy. He was not caught by surprise. He has a plan that is new to me, but it was always well-known to Him. I need to keep my heart and mind open, let His Spirit remind me of His truth, and be open to ideas that come suggesting, "Try this."

We don't have to know where our efforts may lead. At God's command, Abraham left his home, not knowing where he would go. The important thing is to take a step of faith that God will use our willingness to follow our best understanding of His instruction. We can trust the process, knowing God is able to communicate sufficiently in many ways so that we get it.

"And thine ears shall hear a word behind thee, saying, 'This is the way, walk ye in it, when ye turn to the right hand, and when ye turn to the left.'" (Isaiah 30:21)

I know I will have to keep looking and listening for new instructions as my disease progresses. It is day by day. It is the walk of faith that the Bible describes, "As you have received Christ Jesus the Lord, so walk in Him." (Colossians 2:6.) I received Him by mustard seed faith. And it is by faith that I live out each day following Him.

It has been a number of years since my diagnosis, and I have had to give up gardening the way I used to. No more pruning hydrangeas! I have had to minimize activities and limit social functions to conserve energy.

Now I use a walker and a power wheelchair. Changes come progressively, just as the doctor told me they would. But what never changes is God's great love and faithfulness, His wisdom and provision for each day, and His light which illuminates the darkness. And His plan for my life. These form the stabilizing effects in my life and each day.

Changes can be scary, but they can also be exciting, flinging open windows of opportunity that we never imagined. For "God is able to do exceedingly abundantly, beyond anything we can ask or even think, according to the power at work within us." (Ephesians 3:20) He has placed the power—His power!—within us and He will guide us to fulfill the destiny He has designed for us, beyond our imagination. When we realize this and plant our feet on this rock, the dark feelings of helplessness and hopelessness dissolve in the light of His goodness, faithfulness, strength, and truth.

QUESTIONS:

1. Are your conversations, news, movies, music, and reading materials feeding into a sense of futility and hopelessness? Or do they encourage and inspire you?

2. Who or what can help to give you a different perspective than the one you have?

3. Are you reading encouraging material, especially in the Scriptures?

4. What things do others say about your skills and abilities, and things they appreciate about you?

5. How can you put those special qualities to work for someone who needs encouragement? Brainstorm some possibilities and write them here:

STEPS:

1. Identify the source of your hopelessness. If it is based on uncertainty or incomplete information, get the information you need to deal with your situation.

2. Ask God to direct your thoughts.

3. Take stock of your abilities and skills. Make a list.

4. List some options you have. Pray over them as you consider each one.

5. Deliberately focus on God's truth from His Word. Use post-it notes and other reminders to redirect your thoughts when they begin to suggest that nothing will ever change.

6. Use creative outlets to relax your fixated thinking. Art, music, ceramics, woodworking, sewing. These give the brain a rest from stress and allows it to rejuvenate. It is effective therapy.

143

PERTINENT SCRIPTURES:

"May the God of all hope fill you with all joy and peace in believing so that you may abound in hope by the power of the Holy Spirit." Romans 15:13

"Be of good courage, And He shall strengthen your heart, all you who hope in the Lord." Psalms 31:24

"Let us hold unswervingly to the hope we profess, for He who promised is faithful." Hebrews 10:23

"Behold, the eye of the Lord is on those who fear Him, on those who hope in His mercy." Psalms 33:18

"Commit your works to the Lord, and your thoughts will be established." Proverbs 16:3

"If God be for us, who can be against us?" Romans 8:31

"For I know that God works all things together for good to those who love Him and are called according to His purpose." Romans 8:28

"Give, and it will be given to you: good measure, pressed down, shaken together, and running over will be put into your bosom. For with the same measure that you use, it will be measured back to you." Luke 6:38

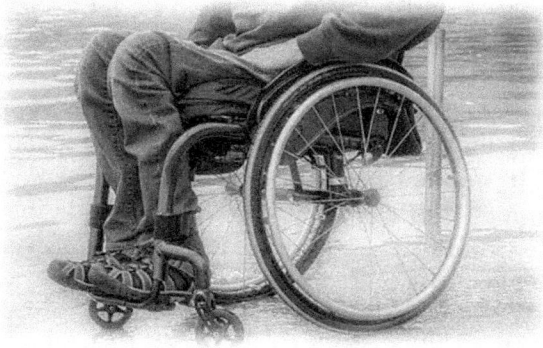

10 Physical Struggles
(with body image, aging, illness, disease, injury)

"I beseech you therefore, brethren, by the mercies of God, that you present your bodies a living sacrifice, holy, acceptable to God, which is your reasonable service." (Romans 12:1)

Through years of singing, giving, listening and reading God's Word, serving in the church, teaching Sunday School, speaking at times to groups of women to encourage their faith, taking an overseas trip for a short-term mission, and other good things that we Christians enjoy doing to better the lives of others, I developed a pretty well-defined picture of what acts of worship are. I had read Romans 12:1-2 many times, and long ago I had decided, rather too quickly, I basically knew what it meant. However, God's Word speaks to us very personally at different times and seasons of our lives, interrupting the comfort of our settled opinions and dogmatic doctrine. It provides us fresh insights to ponder and to bless us. That's what happened to me recently with this wonderful statement telling us to offer God our bodies as an act of worship. It stunned me. I read it over and over, finding new meaning and riches in each phrase, wondering how I had missed them all these years. I marvel at it even now. New thoughts for a new season of life.

What I saw is that this is another way to worship my Lord—by offering my body—in its present form, including its weakness, and its disabilities—as a living sacrifice, holy, and acceptable to God.

ACCEPTABLE?

Honesty compels me to confess that my body has not been acceptable to me for most of my life for various reasons. When I was young, I was deceived into disliking my body because it didn't reflect the "perfect" body image I had in my mind. That attitude was frequently reinforced by media and cultural preoccupations with external appearances. As I approached "middle age" (which I always defined as '10 years older than me' no matter what age I was), my body became even less acceptable to me. "Sagging and wrinkles and fat, oh my!" Another few years, and those fearsome three no longer amused me when I chanted them to the yellow brick road rhythm. That was because reality was unavoidable. It became more difficult to climb stairs, or jog, or go on walks in the woods. I realized things were changing. As the years tick on, my abilities continue to wane.

But my body was formed by God. He knew me and my body before the foundations of the world. Before I was born He oversaw the forming of all my parts while I was in the womb. They included all His plans for me and for my life's purpose. His purpose for me is never thwarted—not even by unexpected (unexpected from my point of view, anyway) events that affect the strength or health or mobility of my body. He knew my DNA would include the gene for muscular dystrophy that would show up late in life while I was making other plans.

"Present your body... acceptable to God." Yes, but how do I make it acceptable to God? As I asked myself this question, I felt a gentle correction. Wherever did I get the idea it is *I* who must make my body acceptable to God? It is already acceptable to Him! He made it the way it is.

God is not interested in my body image the way Hollywood or the media might be. My body is acceptable to Him, apart from any other standard of beauty, size, physical strength or skill levels. He is the potter. I am the clay. Shall the clay say to the potter, 'Why did you make me the way you did?' in an accusing, or fretful way? Such wrong ideas sneak into our unconscious minds subtly, just the way the devil intends them to, through the back door of our thinking. If our wrong ideas about ourselves were quickly obvious we would swat them quickly away with a wave of our hands, like the relentless, distracting, buzzy mosquitoes they are.

Now that I am coping with muscular dystrophy, I must admit that I have asked God, Why did you make my body this way? But it is a curiosity. I desire to know why so that I can cooperate with His plan for my weakening body, a plan I know He has. That is not a bad question to ask with the right reason for asking. Present my body to God? As a living sacrifice? Acceptable unto God? Yes. My body, even with its disabilities, is acceptable to God. Should it not, then, be acceptable to me if I love God and want to become more like His Son? Do I not desire to be able to think as He thinks about things? To see things the way He does? This takes some major readjusting of my perspective, for sure! Some humbling. Some rethinking.

Isaiah gives me a startling challenge regarding who is in charge. As I envision myself as an unformed lump of clay on the Master Creator's pottery wheel, I am told to relax and let the Master's design be formed in me without kibitzing or complaining! Here comes some of that rethinking.

"Surely you have things turned around! Shall the potter be esteemed as the clay; For shall the thing made say of him who made it, 'He did not make me'? Or shall the thing formed say of him who formed it, 'He has no understanding'?" (Isaiah 29:16)

"For you created my inmost being; you knit me together in my mother's womb.

"I praise you because I am fearfully and wonderfully made; your works are wonderful, I know that full well.

148

"My frame was not hidden from you when I was made in the secret place, when I was woven together in the depths of the earth.

"Your eyes saw my unformed body; all the days ordained for me were written in your book before one of them came to be.

"How precious to me are your thoughts, God! How vast is the sum of them!

"Were I to count them, they would outnumber the grains of sand—when I awake, I am still with you." (Psalms 139:13-18 NIV)

The Message offers a more contemporary version of this same passage of Scripture:

"Oh yes, you shaped me first inside, then out; you formed me in my mother's womb. I thank you, High God—you're breathtaking! Body and soul, I am marvelously made! I worship in adoration—what a creation! You know me inside and out, you know every bone in my body; You know exactly how I was made, bit by bit, how I was sculpted from nothing into something. Like an open book, you watched me grow from conception to birth; all the stages of my life were spread out before you, The days of my life all prepared before I'd even lived one day." (Psalms 139:13-18)

No matter what kind of a body I have, or you have, it is to be offered; and it is completely acceptable to God, because He made us according to His design. Pause with me, and think on that for a moment.

HOLY?

I have an automatic reflex reaction to the word holy, thinking that it can't apply to me. I'm not holy. But that's

149

wrong. I *am* holy, because Christ has made me so—through His righteousness and indwelling Spirit. That includes not only my mind and spirit; it includes my body! My body is holy because He has set it apart for Himself. I please God when I agree that my body is holy because He says so! When I consider my body as something I can give Him, my doing so is an act of worship. Previously, I thought of my body as being holy only when it obeyed my bidding, when I chose to act for or towards God in ways I determined—ways *I* thought of as "holy" in my limited and skewed human viewpoint. Wrong! Holy is when I cooperate with God, giving Him total reign over every small act, every attitude, every choice I have (or don't have) that I am tempted to control on my own terms. His reign means my submission, my willingness to do His bidding, no matter how small or insignificant I think it is. It is required of me to be content, to walk by faith and not by sight. It is good to remember that His will is good, acceptable and well-pleasing to Him, as His Word says it is. I have to leave behind my grandiose plans and my own misunderstood standards of what I have labeled "holy" and pay attention to what He, my sovereign God and Creator, says about my body being a holy sacrifice.

SERVICE OF WORSHIP?

"I beseech you, therefore, brethren, that ye present your bodies as a living sacrifice, holy and acceptable unto God, which is your reasonable (spiritual) service of worship." (Romans 12:1)

God offers me an unexpected way to worship Him. It is to offer Him my body, just the way it is, the way He made it, including the way it has changed and aged. It (my body) doesn't seem like much to me. In a way, I feel like the little angel in the classic children's book, *The Littlest Angel,* longing to have something of great value to give Jesus. I don't have much to offer Him. My legs don't work well. My ankles don't bend. My balance is off-center, and I waddle awkwardly when I walk. But I will offer Him what I have. Whatever He can do with what's left of me is gladly given back to Him who gave it to me. He knows what it is capable of, and also what it cannot do.

Recently, God has sent me encouragers from various sources, and I am so thankful for their love, friendship, and kind words. They affirm and encourage me about what I am still able to do, and we have been blessed by what God brings forth as we talk, pray, and laugh together. This is all from the grace of God, and our conversations feel like worship and praise to Him for using imperfect things to honor and enjoy Him.

SACRIFICE?
It is a sacrifice to willingly offer to God what I value and want to control. Money. Position. Reputation. Achievement. Possessions. Self-determination. Control. Misconceptions. Opinions. Valuations. Talents. Intelligence. Skills. All these qualify for sacrifice when I give them to God for His use, regardless of what I believe I can do with them on my terms with my own "inspired" ideas. But there is a higher and more meaningful level of sacrifice according to God's heart. "What I desire" says the Lord, "is the sacrifice of a humble spirit and a contrite heart. These are the sacrifices I desire."

The sacrifices God desires are not what we think they are, or even what we think they ought to be! The sacrifices that God desires are humility, and a willing, contrite heart.

151

He sees the heart of the giver, whether we have much or little to give. When I realize how very little I actually possess to give, but I want to give it to Him, anyway, He receives it as a pleasing and beautiful offering. Jesus pointed this out to His amazed disciples:

"And He looked up and saw the rich putting their gifts into the treasury, and He saw also a certain poor widow putting in two mites. So He said, 'Truly I say to you that this poor widow has put in more than all.'" (Luke 21:1-3)

Jesus' commendation of the widow who gave her very small last coin comforts me a lot. What a reminder that God looks at what we offer Him through the lens of His knowledge of our hearts. "It's not much, but it's all I have" is my thought when I consider offering my body as a "living sacrifice." The widow's coin was not much, but it was all she had. And Jesus was pleased to use it as an important teaching opportunity for His disciples. How ridiculous to think that God would be more pleased if I came to Him, proudly offering Him what I believed was my perfect body? Or even just a "good enough one!" That is just as wrong as thinking I can offer Him a perfect anything! Only He is perfect. I am like the tax collector. "God, be merciful to me, a sinner." He desires a heartfelt offering, even if it seems small in the world's eyes. It is a joyful experience to give to God in faith, believing He sees a heart of love behind it. "God, such as I have, I give thee," is a humble offering, holy and acceptable, pleasing to God.

"O Lord, open my lips, and my mouth shall show forth Your praise. For You do not desire sacrifice, or else I would give it; You do not delight in burnt offering. The

152

sacrifices of God are a broken spirit, a humble and a contrite heart—These, O God, You will not despise." (Psalms 51:15-17)

Thankfulness is an obvious gift we can bring to God. Praise and thanks. How often do I remember to give Him thanks for the many blessings of each day? There is a special book, *1001 Things to Be Thankful For*. Every day has a new array of good things, if we will just pay attention. You might enjoy writing your own version of the book. It will bless you, and it will bless the Lord that you noticed and thanked Him! Thankfulness has an amazing power to reset our negative thinking to a happier frame of mind.

"Therefore by Him let us continually offer the sacrifice of praise to God, that is, the fruit of our lips, giving thanks to His name." (Hebrews 13:15)

SERVICE?
As we age, and are afflicted with weakness, illness, or loss of a limb or functioning, we can become discouraged, thinking we have lost our chances to be of service to the Lord or anyone. I can no longer stand in front of a classroom, or stoop beside a child's classroom desk, or stroll through the playground on recess duty. I cannot go just anywhere I want to. Some places are not accessible to me any longer. I need a ramp, a railing, and wider maneuvering spaces for my walker or wheelchair now. I have to find restaurants, facilities, and shopping areas that are shorter distances if I want to take a friend to lunch or accompany her for ceremonies that I long to show my support for. "The spirit is willing, but the flesh is weak," is no longer just a trite phrase or mild excuse. It is the hard truth for me and others with physical limitations.

153

Service to the Lord is done with our joyful focus oh Him. Other things may be offered to needs around us, but as Jesus said, whatever we do for others, even "the least of these," we have done it as much for Him. Today, due to changes in my life and my physical abilities, my acts of service are much less observable to any potential onlookers. This is just as well. I am not giving service in order to be noticed or rewarded, or even as a perceived obligation. Because I am behind the scenes, I cannot be tempted to seek others' praise for service that should be meant for God's approval alone. Some acts of service, perhaps most, will be invisible to all except Him. We have already mentioned the service of praise and thankfulness. Another is prayer. Our prayers are an act of service that we can offer at any time, any place. What a privilege!

Prayer is a fabulous gift from God to His children. To think that we have unlimited access to the Creator of the universe! It is a stunning realization. He is always listening, always attentive. We don't have to bang on His door or make appointments. We already have His attention. His ears are always open to our prayers.

Prayers are a private act of service. Prayers make a difference in the lives of those we pray for. God sees, knows, and answers our prayers. They make a difference in my life, too. What precious times they are, spending time alone with my God, my Savior, the One who loves me beyond any human love I will ever know. I am certain the times I spend in prayer are quite the richest blessings I can know on this earth. As I pray for provisions, direction, or peace of mind for others, I come away with my own blessings—awareness of His provision and peace, having been reminded of how trustworthy, faithful, and perfect are God's provisions for His children. My burdens are lifted. "Give, and it shall be given unto you, good measure, pressed down, and running over," is just as true for a bedridden or wheelchair-bound praying believer, as it is for anyone running and dancing and climbing and cruising!

There is always hope for those who are eager followers of Christ. He always has a Plan B for us! And it is always good. We only need to be quiet, take time, listen, be willing to seek and find it, asking Him for His guidance and leading. He opens doors and closes doors, using His perfect wisdom and power to make things happen—or to prevent things from happening. We need to learn to trust Him more during that ghastly waiting process that so often is a part of increasing our faith!

I am an impatient one, wanting to see the whole picture, especially the end, before I take my first step to begin the journey. That is not God's way of faith. He tells us to walk by faith, and not by sight. Oh no! You mean I cannot know for sure where I am going? How often that is true. Very often. Usually. In fact, many times when I have stepped out on faith, the direction or plan I think is the one I am destined for somehow evaporates in the process like a desert mirage. I can almost hear our great God chuckling kindly at my consternation! But none of those steps are wasted. God opens the adjacent door, and completes His better plan, in spite of me. How thankful I am that He has an infinite number of ways to accomplish His purpose for me. And many avenues to get me where I am supposed to be!

"Being confident of this, that he who began a good work in you will carry it on to completion until the day of Christ Jesus." (Philippians 1:6 NIV)

"I have learned in everything to be content," writes the apostle Paul. I am learning that, too. Some days I slip and I have to consciously encourage myself in the Lord, as the psalmist David tells us he did during his time of intense stress. We encourage ourselves by remembering how God has come through for us in times past. I have journals that I have written some of these events in. It is encouraging to read them and remember.

I notice as I write about this to encourage you, encouragement is growing in my own heart. How does that work? Writing is one of His gifts. It is a joy to write about the things I've discovered in the depths of God's goodness. I love to share them with others. In the process of communicating it, whether in conversations or in writing like this, I encourage myself by the truths, the experiences I recall, and most especially, by God's Word which is true yesterday, today, tomorrow, and forever. This will be true for you, too. Share with others the upbeat encouraging things you have to be thankful for. As you give away encouragement, you will find it infiltrating your own thoughts and emotions.

It is really amazing that the Almighty God of the universe, Creator of all things, has chosen to indwell His people with His own Holy Spirit. We are indeed like jars of clay, earthen vessels. We chip, crumble, and lose our original external appearance of freshness and beauty that was the source of oohs and aahs at the moment of our birth. Physical strength and beauty, as we all know, is fleeting when measured by the lifespan of most persons living to 70 or 80 or 90 years old. It is a teeny, teeny tiny speck on a timeline that includes eternity. This is reason to have great gladness that our lives do not consist merely of this earth's experience. We stand in awe that Almighty God chooses to indwell us, humble clay pots that we are.

"We have this precious treasure [the good news about salvation] in [unworthy] earthen vessels [of human frailty], so that the grandeur and surpassing greatness of the power will be [shown to be] from God [His sufficiency] and not from ourselves." (2 Corinthians 4:7 AMP)

If I don't feel strong, I must ignore my disappointment and rely on the Word of God which says, "So I am well pleased with weaknesses, with insults, with distresses, with persecutions, and with difficulties, for the sake of Christ; for when I am weak [in human strength], then I am strong [truly able, truly powerful, truly drawing from God's strength]." (2 Corinthians 12:9-10 AMP)

A common mistake we make is when we look at how we are faring today, and begin to worry about how bad it might become tomorrow, or next year. Jesus was well aware of this counterproductive tendency. He included in His sermon on the mount these words, "Don't worry about tomorrow. Sufficient for the day is its own troubles." That is not to warn us that tomorrow is going to get worse! He merely acknowledged that we need to focus on one day at a time when we are prone to think about our difficulties. Our God is a God of hope. That is why Jesus reminded us not to worry about tomorrow. The prophet Jeremiah also gave us God's encouraging words about our future, "For I know the plans I have for you, plans not to harm you but to give you hope and a future." (Jeremiah 29:11 NIV) God wants us to live with hope and confidence in the provision of our faithful heavenly Father. He wants us to be on tip-toe with anticipation.

It was true for Paul, and it is true for you and me. We may not feel strong, but God says that is when His strength comes to us to fill in the gap. We only need to make room for Him with a humble invitation. He will provide all the strength we need to accomplish His purposes for us. Our plans may not be the same ones He has for us, so His strength may come to you in a very different way than you expect. Be alert to His surprising ways. Sometimes they look like coincidences. Nothing is a coincidence when we are praying to our God of hope. He is responsive to our cries for help and guidance. Whatever He does is good and according to His will. He chooses to work in ways that we see His glory, for He is the only one who can work wonders in the most unexpected ways and through the most unexpected people. I think He delights in hearing our oohs and aaahs when He shows up unexpectedly in a glorious display of His power and love. I love those surprises.

"Therefore we do not lose heart. Though outwardly we are wasting away, yet inwardly we are being renewed day by day." (2 Corinthians 4:16 NIV) Do you want to make a difference in this life? You can. You are here. God isn't finished blessing you so you can bless others! Although our physical bodies may be changing, aging, and losing strength, our inner being remains strong and gains strength day by day as we draw closer to God through His Word and prayer. God works His glorious work within our spirits, bringing us His perspective, and giving us greater grace to offer others. Increasing love, joy, and peace by the Holy Spirit transforms us for more godly thinking and attitudes—if we are willing. We will find encouragement for difficult days when we see the invisible things of God that last and we will be rewarded in eternity.

QUESTIONS:

1. How do you view your body? Is it separate or connected to your spiritual life?

2. What do you question God about concerning your physical capabilities?

3. What do you need a better attitude about?

4. Do you believe God can use you just the way you are? Why do you not believe it? Why do you believe it?

5. Do you have a secret dream you have always wanted to pursue? Is now the time?

STEPS:

1. Begin a list or a journal of things you are thankful for today. Don't neglect things that can be easily taken for granted.

2. Choose someone to encourage today. Make a phone call or write a letter.

3. Make a note of people to pray for. Start a prayer journal. Let people know you are praying for them.

4. Look for new ways of doing things to replace activities that are too difficult right now.

5. Investigate a new hobby or interest that you can

learn about or do right now. Visit a library to browse titles in the Hobby section for ideas, information, and inspiration.

6. Invest time in your inner person today. Be renewed by God's Word, praise music, uplifting reading, or giving time to someone who needs you. Do it with the attitude that it is the Lord you are serving, for it is. You will be blessed in the process!

PERTINENT SCRIPTURES:

"But He said to me, My grace is sufficient for you, for my power is made perfect in weakness. Therefore I will boast all the more gladly about my weaknesses, so that Christ's power may rest on me." 2 Corinthians 12:9-10 NIV

"Therefore we do not lose heart. Though outwardly we are wasting away, yet inwardly we are being renewed day by day." 2 Corinthians 4:16 NIV

"But blessed is the man who trusts in the Lord and has made the Lord his hope and confidence. He is like a tree planted along a riverbank, with its roots reaching deep into the water—a tree not bothered by the heat nor worried by long months of drought. Its leaves stay green, and it goes right on producing all its luscious fruit." Jeremiah 17:7-8 TLB

"Being confident of this, that he who began a good work in you will carry it on to completion until the day of Christ Jesus." Philippians 1:6 NIV

160

"For we know that He works all things together for good to those who love Him, who have been called according to His purpose." Romans 8:28 NIV

11 Anger

I have noticed at various times in my life that God gets things done when I'm looking the other way, paying no attention! Do you have a heartache that you have worked to fix, prayed diligently over, even with fasting, sought counsel, tried your best? Me too. To no avail. It was so confusing. I wondered, "Why doesn't God answer me? He knows how much I need His help. I know He has heard every prayer I've prayed, seen every tear I've shed." I felt let down, frustrated, and disappointed.

The issue was my bad temper over little things my little children did. Things that did not deserve a flare-up from me, an outburst of anger for small, childish things that all normal children do. I hated hearing my voice rising and berating them impatiently. Each night I would tuck them into bed, read a story, kiss them, pray with them, and later go back and see their sweet faces resting on their pillows, so innocent and small. As I wept on my knees at their bedsides, I begged God to make me a better mother, to sweep away the impatience and unwarranted anger. The next day I got up full of hope, expecting to be better, but I repeated my same ugly behavior. I was devastated.

This pattern repeated itself for weeks, perhaps longer. I was discouraged, dismayed, and perplexed, knowing God hated my behavior as much as I did. Why didn't He take it away from me? I wanted Him to.

Then an interruption came into the family's routines. Our little church had a new pastor. By way of introducing our small congregation to his teachings, the pastor requested that we set aside several nights during the week for the next several weeks to hear him teach on the working of the Holy Spirit in the lives of believers. We eagerly attended all the meetings. The teachings were thorough and Bible passages were abundant. My husband and I were enthralled. The pastor had many personal examples of startling events, encounters, and people that he was meeting on a daily basis. He was walking the talk. The stories were full of "coincidences," too many to be called coincidences. They were God-ordained people, meetings, and events. All of us were learning more than theory. We were learning how God works in lives that are submitted to Him, as the pastor said, "where the rubber meets the road."

We immersed ourselves in the study passages, and reveled in the teaching each time we met. I cannot say how many weeks went by—perhaps six or more—when I realized that I was no longer weeping over my children after tucking them into bed. I couldn't remember the last time I had lost my temper with them. Somehow, that awful habit had been removed. And amazingly, it was gone forever. I had a new patience level that hadn't been there before. It has carried me through many more seasons of life, situations, and relationships than just that one. I am so amazed and grateful. I am also mystified.

Jesus spoke to Nicodemus about being born again. His description of the spiritual life was done with an analogy, a comparison with the wind.

Jesus answered, "That which is born of the flesh is flesh, and that which is born of the Spirit is spirit. Do not be amazed that I said to you, 'You must be born again.' The wind blows where it wishes and you hear the sound of it, but do not know where it comes from and where it is going; so is everyone who is born of the Spirit." (John 3:6-8)

There are mysterious ways of God that we will not be able to explain. But we recognize a good analogy. The wind is invisible. We feel it on our faces, and we see the results of it in the falling leaves, drifting clouds, and blowing grasses. It moves, and we enjoy it. Similarly, the Holy Spirit moves in us in ways we cannot fully understand. But we can be moved, changed, and experience the blessings of the reality of the Spirit.

I am amazed at how God works, beyond anything I can figure out, ask, or even think. More than once I have seen that one way God works is to get me distracted from the very issues that are troubling me. I often say, "God works in my life in spite of me." I mean it. He sees my failings, my sins, and shows me how they hinder and hurt, so that I will be anxious to be rid of them ASAP. He also shows me that I am incapable of ridding myself of these through my own frantic efforts. I try. It doesn't work. But if I give them to Him for His cleansing, they will eventually be history. He receives all the glory, for He accomplishes these purposes in spite of me. I am willing, I just am not able. He is willing and more than able. He rewards our faith as we trust Him, just like a little child puts her hand in an older hand, and trusts she will be taken safely to her destination.

INSUFFICIENT TIME

One thing I have noticed since becoming a retired teacher is that I have more time these days to accomplish things. A bonus side-effect of that is I also have more patience. It occurred to me today that there is a noticeable correlation among these three things—time, patience, and anger. They are like a mathematical formula.

More time to get something done = more patience.
Less time to get something done = less patience.
More patience = less anger.
Less patience = more anger.

I have noticed that my anger often arises from my impatience, and my impatience comes from feeling the pressure of a deadline, whether self-imposed, or someone else's. This reminds me not to procrastinate or minimize a time frame for getting something completed. Right now, tax preparation is on my list. The filing deadline is only a few weeks away as I write this. I would much rather write than sort through papers and receipts to assemble tax information for the IRS. But if I procrastinate now, I know from past experience that the date will grow more menacing as each day passes on my calendar. If I wait too long, I will get impatient when I am going through receipts and expenses, and I will become angry with myself and anyone or anything I might perceive is interfering with my annual task (my time frame). I will know I am not being fair, but it will happen. So, I will begin the tax filing preparation—today. (Update: I did. And it feels great to have done it without getting impatient or angry!)

INSUFFICIENT SLEEP

Another common source of anger and impatience is a lack of sufficient sleep. Busy families are neglecting the number of hours of sleep that medical professionals tell us is normal and healthy for the human body and brain to recover from life's busy hours and tasks. We are tempted to sacrifice an hour or two of sleep in order to accomplish things that we can't seem to get done during the normal day. I am guilty of this when I am involved in something creative and absorbing, like writing, painting, or designing book covers. I have to be firm with myself to stop at a reasonable hour. It takes intentional planning.

Even minimal sleep loss takes a toll on your mood, energy, mental sharpness, and ability to handle stress. And after a while, chronic sleep loss causes mental and physical health problems. Doctors who have studied the sleep needs of various ages say the average adult needs between 7 and 9 hours of sleep a night. If you are operating on only six hours, it is likely that although you can function adequately on that amount, you are not at your best. 97% of the adult population needs more than six hours a night. Emotions, judgment, coordination, concentration, and reaction times are all affected by sleep deprivation.

Fortunately, this is one area of our lives that we can exert some control over, to improve our emotional resilience and the quality of each day.

PRIDE

Pride is a powerful trigger. I have felt anger beginning to simmer in me when I feel someone is unappreciative, or not accepting my idea, or my instruction. Why do I think my way is the only way, and someone else ought to do it my way? It is pride, plain and simple. Just as there are many routes to get from my home to the school or shopping center, there are ways to do all kinds of things. For me, it is a good exercise in patience and humility to ride alongside my husband in the car and not make suggestions about a better route to take to our destination. It takes self-restraint to keep my mouth shut. It is a reminder to me that I have a strong desire to have things done my way—not a good thing. This is a small example, but it represents my bigger problem—temptation to indulge my self-centeredness and pride.

UNMET EXPECTATIONS

Expectations can set us up for anger. If I am expecting someone to react in a particular way, and it doesn't happen, I may get angry about it. We women are particularly at fault for having expectations of our husbands that they know nothing about. Not knowing the expectation, the husband is likely to overlook it and fail to meet the expectation or desire of his wife. Not because he is inconsiderate. It is just a lack of information. Many men will gladly meet the desire of their wives if they know what it is. How many times have we heard a man say with some exasperation, "I can't read your mind. Please just tell me." This is an honest and fair request. It is my fault when I want others to do something which I haven't even communicated, and then feel disappointed and angry when it doesn't happen. Such anger is very unwarranted and unfair.

DISAPPOINTMENT

Unmet expectations can also come from events, not just from people. People, events, and schedules can disappoint us. Perhaps there is a special occasion or event that is coming up. You make plans for it, and find out that it was last week. You meant to attend, and now it is all over. At first you feel keen disappointment. Then you explode. Disappointment often leads us to look for someone to blame. It can turn to anger at yourself, or some other source that didn't adequately inform you. And you get on the Anger Merry-go-round.

Anger arises from other origins. We think we are angry because of the event. However, often we feel anger as an outward expression of other more hidden emotions. Pride, hurt, disappointment, powerlessness, fear. This is why we are wise to "count to 10" while we think about what is being triggered in our minds and emotions. If we pay attention to the true source of our anger (not a person or an action, but the emotion that underlies it), it becomes more manageable. When things are unclear, they are most hard to combat. Like the swinging at the air with our fists. Isn't it much more gratifying to punch a pillow, something that has substance!

ATTITUDES AND BELIEF SYSTEM

Anger will arise when our belief system is violated. This has both a negative side and a positive side. What is your belief system? It is developed by the guiding principles, behaviors, and experiences we have had from childhood throughout life. As mentioned before, a life that has grown up without a father or mother, or other mature adult as a healthy behavior model is likely to develop anger issues over difficulties that he or she encounters. Without the ability to think through things, or to find constructive ways to compensate for neglect or trauma, one is likely to harbor and act on the anger rather than to think of a solution. The belief system may be "this is how everyone acts," "things won't get better," and "I need to take care of myself, because no one else cares." These attitudes, obviously, are the effects of a negative belief system. They generate anger. It is anger based on bad experiences. As negative experiences increase in number, the belief system becomes more firmly entrenched. Unfortunately, that belief system is not guaranteed to lead to a happy life. It usually leads to a life of anger.

A belief system that is positive can also produce anger. A positive belief system embraces freedom, justice, love, harmony. It is a belief system that has been cultivated by those very elements, which is why we believe them. When a person like this sees an injustice, when innocent ones are harmed, when good seems to be rewarded by evil, the positive belief system is violated. And anger is generated. This is a righteous anger, based on Jesus' teachings to love one another.

Righteous anger can be used for positive results. Many wonderful solutions to social and medical problems have come from individuals who saw injustice or inequality and turned their righteous anger toward forming organizations and outreaches to help others. Incensed by struggles or a lack of provision, inventors and organizers have brought forth new products and services to improve lives.

Righteous anger is evidence of standards that God has given us. In His Word, God tells us that He is angry with evil. "Vengeance is mine," says the Lord, "and I will repay." His wrath will be poured out on the world at the end of time. God, who is perfect, has anger against that which violates His system. But His children will be saved from it, according to His promises.

God tells us "Be angry, but don't sin. Don't let the sun go down with anger and wrath in your heart and mind." Don't go to bed with angry thoughts and attitudes. Ask God for His wisdom and illumination. Recognize your anger for what it is. Determine whether it is righteous anger (based on the teachings of Jesus) or unrighteous (originating from pride, greed, hatred, or another ugly source). Recognize the source of your anger. Don't harbor it. Deal with it. This makes good sense from a medical standpoint, as well. Doctors have long known that unresolved anger as a lifetime habit correlates with diseases such as cancer, heart attacks, and other serious physical conditions. It is healthy to recognize anger and be rid of it as soon as possible each time it raises one of its ugly heads.

When we discover some of the ways we operate and why, we can make changes to decrease the chances of hurting others or even ourselves through needless negative emotions. Especially hurling anger or sarcasm at others who are totally innocent. And particularly children who wonder what on earth they did wrong, when it wasn't about them at all.

I pray for God's perspective. The only way I get God's perspective is to read the Bible. I have many verses in Proverbs about anger that are underlined in lime green. I keep notes on certain things I know I need on a regular basis. If I see the root causes of my anger from His point of view, it sheds new light. My mind becomes transformed, and things don't bother me as they did while I was too busy thinking about how angry I am and things would be much better my way.

There is much more to be said about anger, and whole books are written about working on anger issues. There is a deep form of anger that becomes a state of being. These are serious psychological issues that often require professional counseling to overcome. Examples abound in prisons, where prisoners grew up without fathers (most fall into this category), and have experienced hurt, abuse, violence, injustice, in a disproportional amount. The lack of helpful counsel in their formative years from mature individuals compounds the problem of youths who need perspective, instruction, and comfort. This chapter does not address the deeper issues of living in a state of anger. That is for sociologists, psychologists, and counselors to address.

The point of this chapter is mainly to help us to become aware of some triggers for our temporary anger. We want to make necessary adjustments to reduce the number and degree of occurrences. You may have triggers other than the ones just mentioned. You probably do. Take time to think about what sets you up for sullen withdrawal or angry outbursts. If we know what we are doing and when, it helps. Then we know what we can take to God in prayer, and He will give us greater awareness to understand, pray, plan, and overcome through the power of the Holy Spirit.

Anger can sneak up on us, little by little, as an accumulation of small things. When we begin to notice the small irritations is the time to take notice and think clearly about what is causing them. "Catch the little foxes that spoil the vines." Deal with the problem while it is still small. Don't let it build. Take action against letting things build up. Fall back on a statement you have created to use in such instances. Devise a soft answer statement that you can say in response to a trigger. Something general that will work in most situations. Like, "I will have to think that over." Or simply, "Excuse me. I'll be back in a minute." Or leave the room if you must, to think about it and to keep from escalating the scene.

If your anger tends to grow while you are alone, brooding over an issue, find a distraction. Some people are helped by going for a walk, or just changing their location or activity while the anger subsides. Laughter is always healthy. If you have a collection of humorous sayings or comics, they can be helpful to completely distract your mind from the annoyance you are fighting. We used to resort to *Calvin and Hobbs* comics to do the trick. Singing is another remedy. Somehow, music can pierce the black clouds and bring clarity to our troubles.

I remember trying to fight off a simmering anger against a pastor who misunderstood something I said or did. His misunderstanding caused him to say something to me which shocked and hurt me a great deal. It was a long time ago and I actually don't remember the issue. I only remember the struggle! I prayed and prayed for God to give me a forgiving spirit, and was dismayed that I couldn't make my troubling thoughts and strong defensiveness go away. It went on for days. I knew I needed to forgive, and I tried with all my might, praying for release and forgiveness each time a bad thought came to mind. But the same nasty thoughts kept badgering me, creating unhappy feelings against the pastor. I wanted to be forgiving and forget it all. It wasn't worth the agony. I knew I was wrong to harbor anger, and I was worn out from trying to get back into a joyful attitude. It had been a week of my futile efforts and unending roundabouts of negative thoughts and frantic prayers.

Finally, exasperated, I was ready for anything that would take my mind off it all. I needed a distraction. I went to my sewing machine and began a sewing project that would hold my attention and keep my thoughts from reviewing, ad nauseum, the issue. I couldn't seem to get it out of my mind. I put on some favorite music, a recording of a duet, The Hawaiians. I sewed away on my project, enjoying their songs. Somewhere around the fifth or sixth song, they began to sing about Love. The lyrics were based on the 13th chapter of 1 Corinthians. "Love is…".

I can't explain it, but the lyrics and beautiful harmonizing of their voices were used by God to break through whatever was holding back my unconscious resistance. I crumbled. I wept. I still cannot tell you how it actually happened. I only know that God used music to touch my heart in a way that my mind, my reasoning and thinking, could not. Maybe because my mind was relaxed and thinking about what I was creating, the Spirit had freer access to my heart. I don't know. That seems to describe what I felt. I was totally caught off guard; after a week of struggles, I suddenly was freed of my anger in a moment through two beautiful voices singing about God's love. It was what I needed, a reminder of God's love that I would exercise toward my offender. Everything was fine after that. I was astonished how everything just evaporated into the mist of God's perfect love. I couldn't make it happen, but God could and He did. He works in us both to will and to do His good pleasure.

This is why I often say, "God works in spite of me." I do my best, but my best is not sufficient for the hard stuff. I try to "let go and let God" as the saying goes, and sometimes it is so hard to let go I can't even do that. But because I want to, God's work will not be thwarted. He sees our hearts. He knows what is hindering us and when we surrender it to Him, He will see us through to victory over everything that binds us.

QUESTIONS:

1. What is your belief system based upon? How does your belief system affect your emotions?

2. What mental attitudes and expectations cause you to feel angry? (These are your triggers.)

3. What change in your time schedule can you make to allow that extra time cushion and give yourself fewer triggers to become angry?

4. What is your usual expression of anger (stuffing it, throwing things, yelling, sarcasm, withdrawing)?

5. What alternative action will you take that is healthier for you and those around you?

6. How much will this matter five years from now?

7. Is it worth staying angry?

8. What are you forfeiting while you remain angry?

9. Are you getting sufficient rest and sleep?

10. Are you willing to let go of the anger and the tight stomach, even if you feel your anger is justified?

11. Does your anger originate from hidden feelings of disappointment, fear, unfair expectations, pride, hurt, or powerlessness?

STEPS:

1. Choose a scripture that speaks to you about your anger. Memorize it. Post it where you will see it on a daily basis.

2. While you are retraining your thinking, give yourself permission to walk away from the anger-igniting situation, rather than to react impulsively.

3. Make a plan that you will carry out the next time you feel anger building before anger controls you. A place to go, or an activity that distracts you and gives you time to cool down and gain perspective.

4. Devise a soft answer statement that you will say in response to a trigger. Something general that will work in most situations.

5. Take time to reflect on what God says about anger, and let it influence your decision on how you react.

PERTINENT SCRIPTURES:

"A soft answer turns away wrath, but grievous words stir up anger." Proverbs 15:1

"Do not be quickly provoked in your spirit, for anger resides in the lap of fools." Ecclesiastes 7:9

"The one who has knowledge uses words with restraint, and whoever has understanding is even-tempered." Proverbs 17:27

"Take note of this: Everyone should be quick to hear, slow to speak, slow to become angry because human anger doesn't produce the righteousness that God desires." James 1:19-20

"Love is patient. Love is kind. It is not proud or boastful; It does not dishonor others; it is not self-seeking, it is not easily angered, it keeps no record of wrongs." 1 Corinthians 13:4-5

12   Ghosts of Regrets

We have two major problems with our past—forgetting it, and forgiving ourselves. There are times we feel we don't deserve God's help and intervention today because we remember how we've blown it once or twice or many times before in our past. We want to ask God for His help, but find it hard to believe He has ears to hear us. We erroneously think God might say to us, "If I've told you once, I've told you a thousand times..." or "We've been through this before, haven't we?" A good place to correct this devilish impression is to hear from Jesus' half-brother James about God's actual attitude toward us when we come to Him to ask for His wisdom and guidance:

"If any of you lacks wisdom, you should ask God, who gives generously to all without finding fault, and it will be given to you." (James 1:5)

There is a lot in that verse, but my attention right now is on those three words, *without finding fault*. How marvelous that God will hear us every time without finding fault with us. He never tires of His children coming to Him for help, strength, wisdom, and whatever we need, no matter how many times we have already failed. James tells us simply and directly, what God's response will be—"and it will be given to you." We are welcomed, loved, and provided for.

FORGET IT
"You will surely forget your trouble, recalling it only as waters gone by." (Job 11:16 NIV)

If we have lived any time at all, we have made mistakes. It begins as soon as we can crawl over the edge of the crib and explore the great new world of carpets, puddles, cupboards, drawers, pots and pans, electric cords and sockets, dust bunnies, coffee table edges, books and magazines. We learn as we explore, and we learn a great deal from our mistakes.

The biggest challenge from our mistakes is the challenge of forgiving ourselves from past follies, blunders, and sins. I love the visual I receive from Job 11:16. I picture this:

Water flowing,
    carrying away the troubles and disasters
        of a moment, or a season,

180

"like water under the bridge,"
rippling on downstream,

out of sight,   gone,
replaced by fresh water flowing
today, at this moment
for us right NOW.

We remember
what the water was like
when it was muddy, contaminated, dark.
But that muddy water is gone,
moved downstream by God's outpouring love,
forgiveness, and cleansing,
for a crystal transformation.
Yesterday's dark pools are already overflowing
with new water, continually filled and sweetened
with fresh moving water—again
and again and again—
pushing the murky water
past the horizon
where we can barely remember its existence.

Oh, we remember the lessons learned,
but our present reality only holds those lessons
in a deposit of wisdom along the pebbled bank,
not in an ongoing rehearsal of ugliness that is now
completely washed away.
Our present reality is a gift of fresh water cleansing—
a renewed life—and deep,
deep,
appreciation of God's Grace,
Love, Forgiveness, and glorious Restoration!

ৼৼৼৼৼৼৼ

This is God's provision for us because He knows we need to be free of our past regrets in order to be able to live whole-heartedly, extravagantly, for Him with nothing holding us back. Freedom is God's will for you and me. Putting it into larger context, The Message presents an expanded visual interpretation of Job 11:13-20:

"Still, if you set your heart on God and reach out to him, If you scrub your hands of sin and refuse to entertain evil in your home, you'll be able to face the world unashamed and keep a firm grip on life, guiltless and fearless. You'll forget your troubles; they'll be like old, faded photographs. Your world will be washed in sunshine, every shadow dispersed by dayspring. Full of hope, you'll relax, confident again; you'll look around, sit back, and take it easy. Expansive, without a care in the world, you'll be hunted out by many for your blessing. But the wicked will see none of this. They're headed down a dead-end road with nothing to look forward to—nothing."

God's Spirit clearly conveys through His Word, "His mercies are new every morning." How wonderful it is to have a new day, every day, a new moment, every moment! I need this. This is the contrast between God's redeemed people and people stuck in the world without Him. The Lord is so gracious. He is the Redeemer of all things and of every soul who puts his trust in Him. We must not forget God's words or turn away from them as if they weren't meant for us.

FORGIVE YOURSELF

A common trouble we have is to be able to forgive ourselves. We accept God's forgiveness—who can argue with God—but then we give place to the devil by continuing to wallow in the dirt and ugliness of our past sins, not forgiving ourselves. I believe this is why this proverb is given to us:

"Get wisdom, get understanding; do not forget my words or turn away from them." (Proverbs 4:5 NIV)

If we continue to remember and anguish in our sins, it is the same as if we are actually forgetting God's words or turning away from them. We are arrogantly deciding our own evaluation of our worth—feeling worthless—and ignoring what God says about our sins. He provided forgiveness for them. Not only that—He deliberately, consciously, "remembers them no more." He chooses to "forget"!

When we keep remembering our sins in a way that keeps us mired in the muck of regrets, we are turning away from His words. This is serious. Do not feel you are being exceptionally humble and noble by hating yourself for your past. You are not. You are actually dishonoring the Lord who has done a spectacularly loving act for you, telling you to "just forget it already!" because that's what He has done.

The enemy wants you to dwell in the past. Many times thoughts that badger you are temptations from the enemy to remember things you are meant to let go of. The old saying, "You can't keep the birds from flying over your head, but you can sure keep them from building nests in your hair" is an amusing picture and a good reminder. Temptations do not have to be given any attention. They are only temptations, not your decisions or your completed actions. Don't allow regrets to find a dwelling place in your mind. Fill up that brain room with the glorious truths and reality of God's forgiveness and His complete restoration of you. Declare truth to the enemy as often as you need to until you know you have won. Resist the enemy and he will flee. You will know because you will feel fresh-air freedom!

QUESTIONS:

1. Are you consciously remembering what God says about past sins being gone, gone, gone?

2. Do you feel your sins are too bad for God to forgive? Please read this chapter again.

3. Is it that you believe God has forgiven you, but you cannot forgive yourself? In all love, I beg you to read this chapter again.

STEPS:

1. Go to a moving body of water—stream, river, waterfall—and toss in a leaf. Watch it go downstream until it disappears. Use this visual to impress upon your mind the picture in Job 11:16 "You will surely forget your trouble, recalling it only as waters gone by."

2. Remind God of His Word, and ask Him to make your troubling memories just like water that has passed by and is out of sight, a dim memory, no longer able to trouble you. Your past troubles are meant to provide wisdom now.

3. Read and memorize the Pertinent Scriptures. Receive them without argument. They are Truth and God means them for you.

4. Recognize that the recurring thoughts that you want to be rid of may be the result of demonic suggestions to your mind. It is a temptation from the enemy to get you to dwell on it and feel defeated. Take charge! Speak the truth against the enemy. It is only a temptation, not a habit you will give into. Temptations are ignored and refused in Jesus' name!

PERTINENT SCRIPTURES:

"Get wisdom, get understanding; do not forget my words or turn away from them." Proverbs 4:5

"Forgetting the things that are behind...I press toward the mark of the high calling of God in Christ Jesus." Philippians 3: 13-14

"As far as the east is from the west, So far has He removed our transgressions from us." Psalms 103:12

"I, even I, am He who blots out your transgressions and remembers your sins no more." Isaiah 43:25 NIV

"For I will forgive their wickedness and remember their sins no more." Hebrews 8:12 NIV

"This is the covenant I will make with them... their sins and lawless acts I will remember no more." Hebrews 10:16-17 NIV

"Let us draw near to God with a sincere heart and with the full assurance that faith brings, having our hearts sprinkled to cleanse us from a guilty conscience and having our bodies washed with pure water." Hebrews 10:21-22

13   Divorce Aftershocks

God works with broken people. How thankful we are that we are not "throw-away toys," when we become dented, damaged, broken, and feel like useless and unacceptable failures. We all have these feelings when situations in life have been trying, traumatic, and unmanageable. But they must not be allowed to become our identity.

The thoughts expressed in this chapter are not ones I have developed as a personal agenda. I am not divorced. But I have seen the awful pain and injustice that believers have heaped on their brothers and sisters while taking positions on the issue of divorce and remarriages of divorced people. It surely must grieve the heart of God when we inflict further damage and heartache on a divorced person. This inconsistency with the heart of forgiveness that God clearly expresses in His Word creates what psychologists call "cognitive dissonance," two contradicting messages that require a shift in thinking and new attitudes in order to resolve the conflict. God sent His Son for us to have life, and have it more abundantly. Christ is our burden bearer, not our accuser and executioner.

Others who have studied the scriptures and devoted many hours to learn about the background of the culture and practices of the time are arriving at these same convictions. Their conclusions and the ones I express here are based solely on the desire to reconcile scriptures that have been separated from their context and erroneously applied to divorced and divorcing individuals, causing unnecessary anguish and harm. It is my solemn and sincere desire to deal with this subject in order to remind us that the overall message of our heavenly Father to His beloved children is one of love, forgiveness, healing, and redemption.

A whole host of negative emotions are involved in any divorce. You may be experiencing the aftershocks of divorce. Or you may be feeling the first warning shakes of an impending divorce-quake, and are wading through the quagmire of emotions that are involved. Divorce is a time of negativity, shock, fear, confusion, betrayal, and low self-esteem. The emotional rubble cannot be easily navigated, partly because of the lack of experience of others who want to comment, help, or "fix" you. Partly because of how friends and family members redistribute themselves by taking sides between you and your spouse. Partly because of poor counsel given by those who think they know, but don't really understand how devastating the pressure buildup was and how lingering the aftershocks are. And, sadly, partly because of misunderstood scriptures that are applied cavalierly as a blanket of generalization to every divorce situation, without regard to the background of the scriptures that are glibly quoted, and without regard to the individual circumstances involved.

Because of the complexity of emotions, this chapter is devoted to thinking through some of the confusion, in order to reduce the effects of misplaced shame, regrets, and condemnation. I hope these scriptures and reflections will help you sort through and resolve some of the emotional rubble. Don't be fearful of encountering judgment, condemnation, or rejection. You won't find them here.

What this chapter holds is scriptures and principles concerning the love of God and His purpose for our lives, along with some answers to well-meaning people who have misapplied individual verses of scripture by isolating them from their context. This chapter will encourage you to remember that God's intention for you is to experience His presence, His love, His forgiveness, His provision, and His peace. Sadly, much Christian teaching on divorce has overlooked the over-all grand principle that God has given us above all others—that is, the truth of God's passionate desire for His creation—you and me—to have a close relationship with Him, which embodies all of the components just listed, plus so much more. The entire Bible is all about God who seeks and enjoys personal relationships with each of His creation, men and women. This is as true for divorced people as it is for singles and couples. A divorced person is not in a separate category.

I think we can all agree on the necessity of reading God's Word and meditating on it in the context of the whole counsel of His Word. It is dangerous and heresy-prone for anyone to take a single statement from the Bible and build a dogmatic case on a small segment of a larger truth. Any single portion of God's Word will fit with the entirety of God's wonderful revealed Word in the scriptures, and it all needs to be considered together. If we are not watching for that when we read any particular passage, we will wrongly try to put a single verse into the context of our own specific culture, limited experiences, assumptions, and current set of beliefs when it doesn't belong there. And we will add to the emotional distress that is already consuming the troubled mind and spirit. This happens much too often, and needlessly.

To avoid misinterpreting what God says and means for us to live by today, we must take time to study, pray, and search the counsel of God, comparing scripture with scripture, and keeping in mind the culture, issues, and habits of the 1st century AD, and earlier. Our purpose is to understand the truth of what God has given us in His Word, not to justify a position that we have read, heard, or spoken. We just want to understand as best as possible what the will of God is for us in any given situation. Not a rule to be followed. But a heart to be heard. We want to be like the people in Berea. "These were more fair-minded than those in Thessalonica, in that they received the word with all readiness, and searched the Scriptures daily to find out whether these things were so." (Acts 17:11)

A fascinating question came to my mind the other day that propelled this study. It was, "What cultural convictions controlled the minds of the people to whom

Jesus spoke regarding divorce?" That was 20 centuries ago—a long time! Jesus would be speaking to them in connection with their lives then. I have been asking for God's point of view as I read and pray, because it is a troubling issue for many denominations and individuals seeking to please God and to follow Him in all their ways, including divorce-related issues. Why is it such a controversial topic?

Naturally, some things are eternal, and will be applicable to all cultures, throughout time—such as the nature of God, His purity, His power, His beauty and perfection, His love, mercy, justice, and grace. But we know there are other things that are unique to man's cultures around the world, with wide variations in human preferences, opinions, and habits. These have no bearing on salvation or God's unchangeableness. To keep these distinctions—man's variableness and God's unchanging character—prayerfully in mind requires a stern exercise of mental discipline and open-mindedness without compromising central truths about God and His plan and will for all mankind.

In the years preceding Christ, historical documents, scriptures, and Jewish laws reveal that a man was allowed to divorce his wife for any cause, simply at the husband's whim. Wives were discarded, put away for superficial reasons, even for spoiling the supper's broth. All a disgruntled husband needed to do was get a certificate of divorce, sign it, and it was done. Women had no say in the matter. The husband was free and the wife was sent away to fend for herself. It was unjust, unloving, and evil in God's sight. I am glad that our loving God looked upon this and hated it. Knowing this provides us a context we might not otherwise consider.

Regarding divorce today, the phrase "God hates divorce" is often thrust into the conversation. It is not as simple and cut-and-dried as all that. We need to take care to consider all of what God says about relationships, approving marriage, and hating divorce, and realize that God's Word is a multi-faceted diamond of love and truth, mercy and grace.

In this chapter I want to go beyond the quick and easy, sometimes flippant, answers that Christians give concerning divorce. I will offer some scriptures to help clarify the issues you may be dealing with. You may have heard well-meaning people insist you violated God's will. However, as the old song goes, "It ain't necessarily so."

IT'S ALL ABOUT THE HEART

God has a high standard, but He does not have a Checklist of Rules that we go down, check, check, check. It is not about our works, what we do. When Christ taught about keeping the law, commandments, and how to please God, he highlighted the heart. It became maddeningly clear to the religious rulers of the time that God's attention goes deeper than outward appearances and man-made standards of valuation. When God sees us, His evaluation goes to the deepest interior spaces of our hearts.

An illustration of this is when God sent the prophet Samuel to find and anoint a new king for Israel. Samuel quickly jumped to conclusions, and thought he could identify the new king.

But the Lord said to Samuel, "Do not consider his appearance or his height, for I have rejected him. The

Lord does not look at the things people look at. People look at the outward appearance, but the Lord looks at the heart." (1 Samuel 16:7)

The Lord God corrected Samuel each time until he selected the right one, the youngest, the one with a heart for God—David. In every one of us, God sees our hearts. He knows the agony and ecstasy of each one. He knows what we can tolerate. He knows what we thrive on. He knows what will destroy us. His knowledge is not scary. It is comforting, because when no one else understands us, He does. And He is not critical. He is patient with His children, tenderly correcting and instructing.

Consider Matthew's gospel, Chapters 5, 6, and 7. It takes three chapters of the Bible to share the stunning words of Jesus during His sermon on the mount. The three chapters need to be read together as one section, because the thoughts are from a single time and event. Each portion should be thought about in the context of the entire message Jesus gave to the mixed crowd gathered on the hillside. You might want to take the time to read these three chapters right now...

God's ability to see and know the heart of any of us at any time, all the time, has a bearing on the divorce issue. Jesus' teaching touches the very soul and spirit of man. Looking at a woman with lust is the equivalent of adultery. Anger is the equivalent of murder. If your hand steals, cut off your hand. Love your enemy, turn the other cheek. What in the world does this mean to us? Obviously, it shows us, from the very mouth of the Lord, that He is most concerned about the state of our hearts, because whatever we do or say originates first in our hearts and minds. What is the attitude of my heart? Is it to serve God, to please Him? To love others? Or am I hoping to "get by" through doing things which make me look good, going through the motions, teaching Sunday School, visiting the sick, singing in the choir, leading a prayer?

These outward appearances mean nothing to God. He looks deeply into the heart. This is imperative to remember when considering what it means when God says He hates divorce! Why does He hate divorce? Does He hate it simply because a man and woman can no longer live together under one roof? Or is there a deeper message in it all?

There is a deeper message. No issue with God is an isolated issue. It always is in the context of His love and plan for your life. God is FOR you. God is FOR good and right relationships between men and women, his children. He is FOR good and right relationships between Himself and His children. The latter is of the utmost importance to God. Relationship between man and God is why He sent His only begotten Son to earth to live and die for us. There is a great divide between man and God because of our sin. But God's provision of Jesus' substitutionary death brings us into relationship with Him once again, when we place our faith in His love and gratefully receive His sacrifice for our sins. What amazing love! We err very greatly when we ignore this aspect of God's character, His very being. It needs to be the context for everything else God says in His Word.

THE CENTRAL ISSUE

The topic of our value to God and the salvation He has given us is not a digression in this conversation. It is central to finding truth and peace of mind about divorce. The obvious, comforting truth in Christ's sacrifice is that our life in Christ is the most valuable and significant aspect of any part of our lives here on earth. It extends into eternity, forever and ever. If, against all my efforts to the contrary, someone has come between me and God, and is causing my spiritual life to sicken and die a slow, agonizing death of abuse or neglect, it is, unquestionably, God's will that I avoid—even remove myself from—such an evil. God hates divorce. It represents the end of something God intended for blessing. But He hates even more our separation—the great divide—from His glory, His life, and His purpose for our lives.

What does He value most highly? This answer is an easy one. He values what His Son's blood purchased. Our redemption. Our new life. He values us most highly. Whatever interferes, prevents, erodes, or destroys that precious blood-bought relationship is something that must be resisted and fought off. It is a war for our soul and spirit!

ANALOGIES

The Old Testament reference to "God hates divorce" in Malachi 2:16 is quoted from the analogy God gave to Malachi. It's absolutely necessary to read the book of Malachi to get the context. We can then see that God is using Malachi to speak to His people the Jews about their rebelliousness against God. The divorce in this passage is between God and His people, their idolatry, their spiritual rebellion, coming between them and God. God hates separation from His people—the departure of their hearts from His. That is what Malachi is all about. We are wrong to assume it is primarily God's statement about men and women divorcing. God gave the divorce analogy to Malachi to impress upon His people the great division and grief that God feels when His people turn their backs on Him. To reverse that thought and say God hates divorce between men and women, and, by the way, God also hates it when we rebel against Him, is totally backwards.

God gives us comparisons and examples from our physical lives in order to help us understand truths that are in the spiritual realm. Similar to Malachi's analogy, God gives us an analogy in Revelation 2:4. "Nevertheless I have this against you, that you have left your first love." In this case, He is speaking about the spiritual church's first love, Christ. He is not speaking about individuals. And he is not speaking about an earthly love between earthly individuals. However, we understand the meaning of the statement based on our earthly experiences. It would be an error to extrapolate that we sin against God when we leave our earthly first love. My earthly "first love" was at age 15. He was definitely not one God would approve of me marrying and spending the rest of my life with! In fact, in hindsight, neither would I! Sometimes it's good when we leave our "first love." So, it is clear that is not what Revelation 2:4 is talking about. It is an analogy.

One more example. God the Father sent us His Son, Jesus, Immanuel, "God with Us." He told us, "This is my beloved Son," and we understand because of our earthly relationships with our own children how dear and precious Jesus, God in the flesh, was, and is, to God the Father. God also gave us earthly children, so that we can understand how passionately He cares about you and me, His born-again ones. Believers in Christ are called "children of God" and "sons of God." Obviously, we are

196

not literally God's children in the physical sense. We were not born of a virgin, like Jesus was. God makes these earthly analogies and comparisons to give us greater understanding of spiritual principles and truths about Him that we otherwise would have no idea of. We must be careful not to pluck out analogies and metaphors and apply them inappropriately according to our preset views.

Do you see how analogies in scripture must be kept in their context? Cults occur when individual verses are taken out of context and used to stand alone for certain agendas and dogmas, distorting the truth.

IF IT IS POSSIBLE

Divorce. Of course God hates the schism, the lack of love. It grieves Him when His creation wreaks strife instead of harmony. This will always be true in any circumstance, including anger, bitterness, unforgiveness, grudges, lying, betrayal, all of which may have been involved in the divorce, but also occur in other situations. These grieve and quench the Spirit. So we do all we can to maintain and nurture the marriage relationship as much as we can for as long as we can.

"If it is possible, as much as depends on you, live peaceably with all men." (Romans 12:18) If it is possible. As much as depends on you. These are crucial parts of the instruction and exhortation to live peaceably. Sometimes the limits are reached. We cannot control the actions of others. Sometimes there is physical danger. Sometimes there is emotional damage that is far-reaching. Sometimes there is great spiritual conflict that robs the home and family of peace, safety, love, and well-being. Sometimes there is rebellion on the part of one who refuses to submit to the loving power and will of God, regardless of all that the other spouse gives, does, and prays.

Does God demand that the injured spouse (emotionally, physically, or spiritually injured) stay indefinitely under the shroud of rebellion and evil that he or she has not been able to change or avoid? What must he or she do to keep an environment of evil from hindering, harming, or enslaving her? What is the cost of staying in an evil, oppressive situation, living in fear and anxiety instead of love and grace? Does God want us to forego His redemptive plans for us and live under the weight of darkness and fear because of a time in our lives when we trusted the flippant promises, the casual vows, of an uncommitted heart that deceptively led us to believe we were following a right path? No. God is our Redeemer, not our prison guard.

AUTHENTICITY

Let's revisit the heart issue. Jesus always saw things exactly as they were, in spite of a person's hypocritical efforts to deceive. In the New Testament, a peculiar grace—one that far exceeds human "goodness"—enters the scenario.

Why do I call it a "peculiar grace?" Because it so far exceeds what man's imagination at its very best would come up with as an example of grace. In the sermon on the mount, Jesus shows us that God has very high standards. In fact, the standard is perfection. Can anyone meet that standard? Of course not. Only Jesus met that standard, because He is God and it was His own standard. What Jesus was pointing out was our need for Him! We need the Savior! We need the forgiveness God freely offers us if we will but humble ourselves and ask. This is the peculiar grace—one only God could devise and declare just and good, and put into practice through the spectacular gift of His Son's sacrifice on our behalf.

The standard in the New Testament is not only about our actions, keeping the Old Testament law. Jesus' New Testament teaching is about our attitudes and thoughts, the condition of our spiritual hearts! Jesus wants us to realize God's perfect heart! His life of love, healings, compassion, and sacrifice demonstrated it. Jesus gives us insight into God's standard for the heart, but not to burden us with an impossible set of rules to follow. The examples are to reveal to us what is important to God. It is not rules and laws, but attributes the Holy Spirit brings to our lives in Christ—love, joy, peace, longsuffering, kindness, goodness, faith, gentleness, and self-control. If we have these, the appropriate actions follow. When we are responding and exercising the gifts of the Spirit, there is no room for anger, bitterness, condemnation, and punishment.

God is not impressed by actions that do not have a corresponding heart attitude of love, graciousness, and selflessness. He makes this plain in Matthew 7:21-23. It is a sobering report of people coming to Christ, calling Him "Lord" and saying they prophesied in His name, they cast out demons in His name, and performed wonders, all in the name of Jesus. But Christ has a sobering answer to them. "I never knew you. Get away from Me. You practice lawlessness." What was He saying? Why was He so bluntly commanding in sending them away? Because He saw through the outward façade, right into their hearts.

Jesus had just finished telling the crowd about being aware of deceitful ones, false prophets who come in

199

sheep's clothing, but who actually are ravenous wolves. They will become known by their fruits, he said. He had also just said, "Do not give what is holy to the dogs; nor cast your pearls before swine, lest they trample them under their feet, and turn and tear you in pieces." (Matthew 7:6) There are deceivers who will not appreciate the grace you extend to them. Their hearts will not be touched by your love, your pearls, your words of encouragement, your selfless acts. These are like ravenous wolves, dogs, swine, living for themselves; and we are told not to give out our precious treasures for them to trample. Precious treasures of God's life, love, truth, comfort, and graciousness.

We are told to turn the other cheek. That doesn't mean we can't walk away. It only means not to strike back. It means not to become like them, not to be pulled down to their level. We must turn away from evil. See what Timothy wrote:

"But know this, that in the last days perilous times will come: For men will be lovers of themselves, lovers of money, boasters, proud, blasphemers, disobedient to parents, unthankful, unholy, unloving, unforgiving, slanderers, without self-control, brutal, despisers of good, traitors, headstrong, haughty, lovers of pleasure rather than lovers of God, having a form of godliness but denying its power. And from such people turn away!" (2 Timothy 3:1-5)

Timothy gives strong words to Christ's followers, instructing us to pay attention to the influences and influencers in our lives and to turn our backs on destructive ones. Note that the list includes those who have a "form (façade) of godliness." Denying the power of godliness is a tip-off. Plenty of talk, but no walk. Not real. Not good.

Now for an important detail. When we read the sermon on the mount in Matthew's gospel, Chapter 5, we must not take all of it literally. Jesus used dramatic word pictures to make His points to His listeners. Verses 29 and 30 are startling. Here they are:

"If your right eye causes you to sin, pluck it out and cast it from you; for it is more profitable for you that one of your members perish, than for your whole body to be cast into hell. And if your right hand causes you to sin, cut it off and cast it from you; for it is more profitable for you that one of your members perish, than for your whole body to be cast into hell." (Matthew 5:29-30)

If we were to take the literal application of all the examples Jesus gave, it would mean we would be a whole population of one-eyed, one-handed folks groping around neighborhoods and city streets, and huffing and puffing down that second mile—that is, if we weren't on death row for murder! Applying these words literally would be a giant step forward in population control, for sure. It's not exactly laughable, but surely you see the ludicrous implication of a literal interpretation. It is clear from Jesus' words that we are to regard the ultimate health of the whole body and soul to be in great danger from even a single permitted destructive element. A compromised, single evil element must be identified, conquered, and removed, in the interest of rescuing the overall life. Jesus' words were dramatic, to make His point clear and memorable. He even repeats it to make sure we get it. Remember, this is all in the same sermon that Christ gave in one sitting. Keep it all together, in context.

What happens when a Christian finds herself in a relationship that began differently, but now has changed, exposing her to sinful practices and destructive demands? Paul writes an instruction in his first letter to the Corinthians. Paul was a spiritual mentor to Timothy and it sounds a lot like Timothy's words:

"But now I have written to you not to keep company with anyone named a brother, who is sexually immoral, or covetous, or an idolater, or a reviler, or a drunkard, or an extortioner—not even to eat with such a person." (1 Corinthians 5:11)

What happens when it becomes evident that such a person is a marriage partner? What does God expect? Does God set aside his sovereign plan, His primary desire for His child's life, simply because a ceremony was performed at some time in that person's experience, declaring a union in an earthly relationship? If so, how do we ignore the biblical counsel not to keep company with someone like that—named a brother, who is sexually immoral, or covetous, or an idolater, or a reviler, or a drunkard, or an extortioner? It is a contradiction. Paul writes, don't even eat with such a person.

These are not easy questions to answer if we try to apply "one size fits all." The vulnerable or injured spouse must seek the counsel of the Holy Spirit for her particular situation and ask how it is affecting her relationship with God. God is faithful. He answers the desperate cries of a sincere heart who seeks to follow Him. He is a loving, wise, protective Father.

CLEAR ANSWERS

There actually is a clear answer when all of God's Word is taken into account and a divorce scripture is not isolated from the rest of scripture. Above all, God wants His people to glory in Him, and put Him above all earthly persons, things, and situations. Most of all, he wants us to know Him, that He is the Lord, who exercises and delights in lovingkindness, judgment, and righteousness: "Thus says the Lord:

'Let not the wise man glory in his wisdom,
Let not the mighty man glory in his might,
Nor let the rich man glory in his riches;
But let him who glories glory in this,
That he understands and knows Me,
That I am the Lord, exercising lovingkindness, judgment, and righteousness in all the earth. For in these things I delight.'" (Jeremiah 9:23-24)

So, what about Jesus' words on divorce during His sermon on the mount? "Furthermore it has been said, 'Whoever divorces his wife, let him give her a certificate of divorce.' But I say to you that whoever divorces his wife for any reason except sexual immorality causes her to commit adultery; and whoever marries a woman who is divorced commits adultery." (Matthew 5:31-32)

We remember the mindset of the time, and the accepted cultural standards. He is addressing the held-over easy-divorce Old Testament permission with which all His audience was familiar in His time and culture. Remember, it was an easy action that a husband could take to get rid of a wife who displeased him in any way. Jesus contrasts that now with the clear statement "But, I say to you…" to show a mere stroke of a pen on a certificate of divorce is

203

an insufficient and unacceptable action for such a serious and callous decision. He emphasizes the importance and significance of joining together as husband and wife. It is not to be taken or treated lightly. God cares about marriage. That is plain. Jesus essentially said, "Forget about a handy-dandy certificate of divorce. Be sure there is a legitimate reason, something as serious as sexual immorality—which causes a damaging severing of the relationship in which the covenant has been obviously violated and severed—before even thinking about divorce." In other words, carefully consider what you are thinking (look at your heart attitude!) before you take such a drastic action.

Why would Jesus say, "Except sexual immorality" as the only reason divorce is acceptable? What about the danger of physical or emotional injury? Are these issues obvious enough that Jesus did not need to name them? Are they covered by other clear dictates, such as the need for safety? I think so. Certainly the Lord does not expect any of His children to stay with a violent partner and become a victim. Violence is spoken of many times in the Bible. It is despised and to be avoided. It is not that God is unaware of its existence! Issues like these require prayer, help, and counseling for the one who is in a frightening, damaging, or threatening situation. Reasonable and wise counsel will say, "Leave." Certainly, get to safety.

Sadly, even these situations are not always understood and supported by church members and denominations. For much more in-depth study of the historical and cultural practices at the time of Jesus, which He was addressing, you will find helpful details *in Divorce and Remarriage—A Redemptive Theology*, by Rubel Shelly.

David, in King Saul's court, was subjected to Saul's insane violent behavior, and David left for his own safety. He was not wrong to do so. He suffered, but maintained his integrity and trust in the Lord until the Lord completed His plan and placed David on the throne He had ordained for him. The Holy Spirit will be your guide. Follow His leading, His counsel, and His encouragement to take steps to become free of violence, oppression, and evil. You have the heart of God to undergird your actions.

It is tempting to want to make things "easy" and write a one-size-fits-all biblical rule about divorce. But it is apparent that one size wasn't the intent of the Lord Jesus. He clearly establishes the solemnity of marriage. But at the same time, He speaks of cutting off whatever interferes with or prevents the all-important sovereign purpose of God for His child's life. A redeemed life is not to be thrown away in order to accommodate a spouse's evil influence or destructive indulgence. The redeemed one was bought by the precious blood of Jesus Christ. That costly life is valuable beyond description and is not meant to be desecrated through vile treatment or purpose.

SALT AND LIGHT
Then what should be the attitude of the church on divorce? It should be the attitude of Christ. We are not defined in God's eyes by any single action or decision. Life is more than any one single event. The Lord sees our whole timeline; in fact, He has given us each minute, hour, and year on that timeline. He has a plan for our lives. None of us will live life perfectly. There are far too many pitfalls, potholes, and sinkholes to recognize. We will not see them all, especially if we are walking in the dark. And there are times in our lives when it's dark, very dark. We

don't see it coming, just as Eve didn't see the seriousness of just taking one little bite.

The wonderful, matchless truth is that God's grace is extended to His creation—men and women—time after time, for more than a single wrong decision, wrong turn, wrong event. The blood of Jesus covers every sin of the entire world, and forgiveness and grace is freely given to each of God's frail children, stumbling along, learning, doing the best we can, and ever so gratefully receiving the all-inclusive, unconditional love of the Father through His Son Jesus each time we blow it, whether by weakness or by deception. He sees our motivations, our attitudes, our hearts. We are important to Him. He knows our strengths and He knows our weaknesses. It is because of our sins and weaknesses that He came, not because of our strengths. His strength is made perfect in our weakness. What a Great and Glorious God! Hallelujah!

It is God's design that we become salt and light, a beautiful influence in the world. This is our calling, not to cower in fear and subjection to darkness, sometimes cloaked in bad theology, power struggles, and condemnation. Jesus speaks of the design God has for us to glorify Him. We are to "walk in the light, as He is in the light." (1 John 1:7)

"You are the salt of the earth; but if the salt loses its flavor, how shall it be seasoned? It is then good for nothing but to be thrown out and trampled underfoot by men. You are the light of the world. A city that is set on a hill cannot be hidden. Nor do they light a lamp and put it under a basket, but on a lampstand, and it gives light to all who are in the house. Let your light so shine before men, that they may see your good works and glorify your Father in heaven." (Matthew 5:13-16)

To summarize, regarding divorce in the context of God's purposes, His love, and His Word to us over the centuries:

- God's will is for us to have a close personal relationship with Him.
- God's desire and plan is to strengthen and grow our relationship with Him.
- We are to resist evil and forces that oppose a growing and thriving relationship with God.
- Marriage is meant to be a blessing to God's people.
- Marriage is meant to reflect Christ's love for the church, and the church's submission to His Love.
- Marriage is God's design to describe His covenant relationship between God and His people.
- An injured spouse is not asked or required by God to stay in an environment where his or her spirit is eroded by unrepentant evil, or other danger.
- We are to walk in the light as He is in the light.

God alone is the one who sees the hearts of those involved. We are required to answer to Him above all others. He knows and guides by His Holy Spirit for the good of His children. When He gives direction to the humble and sincere heart that seeks Him, we must not pass judgment based on man's denominational rules or personal opinion. The divorcing or divorced man or woman will receive comfort and reassurance from the Holy Spirit as they humbly seek His truth in spite of opposition from those who don't understand.

"O Lord, open my lips, and my mouth shall show forth Your praise. For You do not desire sacrifice, or else I would give it; You do not delight in burnt offering. The sacrifices of God are a broken spirit, a broken and a contrite heart—These, O God, You will not despise." (Psalms 5:15-17)

"[God says]For I desire mercy and not sacrifice, and the knowledge of God more than burnt offerings." (Hosea 6:6)

"Thus says the Lord:
'Let not the wise man glory in his wisdom,
Let not the mighty man glory in his might,
Nor let the rich man glory in his riches;
But let him who glories glory in this,
That he understands and knows Me,
That I am the Lord, exercising lovingkindness,
judgment and righteousness in all the earth, for in
these I delight,' says the Lord." (Jeremiah 9:23,24)

Please identify false teaching, wrong counsel, and misapplied scriptures that may have fueled your sense of failure and condemnation. Let go of them by consciously redirecting your thoughts and focusing on God's truth. Walk in the light. Life with Christ—walking by faith and not by sight—begins with knowing that God sees, understands, forgives, provides, heals, and makes all things new. When we walk by faith it is the same faith that we used when we placed our faith in Him for our salvation. When we received Him as Lord, we submitted in humility and gave Him rule over our lives. To "walk in Him" means we continue to submit everything to Him, the visible things we cherish and the invisible things in our

208

hearts and minds that we know need His touch. Entrust your past, present, and future to Him. He loves you beyond your wildest imagination. Not just to the moon and back.

To the moon and beyond, into all eternity.

QUESTIONS:

1. Are you suffering under teaching that is not rooted in Scripture?

2. What does God see when He looks at your heart? Is there a contrite and humble spirit?

3. What kind of negative thoughts have you allowed into your thinking that you know God wants to bring His healing to?

4. If you have been hurt by others' lack of support of

your current situation, what words from Jesus are the greatest comfort to you?

5. Are you willing to forgive those who have caused you pain over your divorce issues? (Ex-spouse, family members, friends, pastors?)

6. Are you blaming God for what you have experienced from believers who have acted and spoken in ignorance of correct interpretation of scriptures?

7. Do you recognize that God's loving grace is the overall umbrella for your life—past and future?

STEPS:

1. Soak in God's Word about His love for you, and His grace. A good review of this will be to read the Gospel of John.

2. Remind yourself that the sacrifices God desires are not the traditional things we think about. It is a humble and teachable spirit, a thankful heart, a heart that seeks Him first. These please Him above all that we do.

3. Resolve to forgive those who have hurt you. Lack of forgiveness becomes bitterness and will do more damage to your life. Holding onto pain and anger isn't worth it.

4. Find a church that understands and accepts all hurting people, including divorced ones, as loved ones of God. Serve in a volunteer capacity and meet others who

have experienced God's love and restoration from His people. This can be a time-consuming exploration, but God will lead you to His place for you among believers who understand and welcome you.

PERTINENT SCRIPTURES:

"Our conscience testifies that we have conducted ourselves in the world, and especially in our relations with you, with integrity and godly sincerity. We have done so, relying not on worldly wisdom but on God's grace." 2 Corinthians 1:12

"In him we have redemption through his blood, the forgiveness of sins, in accordance with the riches of God's grace." Ephesians 1:7

"Let us then approach God's throne of grace with confidence, so that we may receive mercy and find grace to help us in our time of need." Hebrews 4:16

"Surely it was for my benefit that I suffered such anguish. In your love you kept me from the pit of destruction; you have put all my sins behind your back." Isaiah 38:17

"Truly I tell you, people can be forgiven all their sins and every slander they utter." Mark 3:28

"The grace of the Lord Jesus be with God's people. Amen." Revelation 22:21

14 How to Surrender Negative Emotions

Have you ever hugged someone who wasn't accustomed to hugs? They felt stiff and unyielding. You knew right away that the "huggee" didn't feel comfortable and didn't know exactly how to hug back. Have you ever been given a hug that you didn't want? Hugs don't work very well when they are one-way hugs. However, you have probably received a warm hug when you desperately needed one. Somehow, a hug takes care of a lot of hurt when we are ready to accept it.

Have you ever had a shoulder rub, foot massage, scalp massage, or muscle massage of any kind? Remember how soothing it was to your sore muscles and even a tense frame of mind? Didn't it bring relief that was not only physical, but also emotional? Perhaps it even lifted your spirits afterwards, removing tired and tense muscles and worrisome thoughts at the same time.

We can experience similar relief of comfort and hope from God. After we have wrestled continually with our all too familiar enemies of helpless or hopeless feelings, we feel exhausted and need relief. How do we rid ourselves of these, really, in order to receive God's comfort and hope?

We receive God's comfort, hope, love, and reassurances the same way that we receive a hug. The same way we receive a muscle massage. By surrendering, and letting it come to us. I remember my first ever session in massage therapy. My muscles were so tight and sore. Nothing I had done at home or in the gym was helping some trouble spots throughout my body. I wasn't particularly comfortable psychologically with having my muscles kneaded by a stranger. I didn't know the massage therapist until I walked through the door of her clinic. I was more tense than ever, not knowing how the session would go. I didn't know if the massage would help or hurt me more. Friends had recommended her to me, extolling her skillful, respectful, and caring approach, but I had to consciously surrender my reluctance in order to relax and receive the benefit of the session.

Isn't this also true of a hug? In order to receive the comfort and benefit of a friendly hug when we are suffering, we have to surrender our reluctance and admit our vulnerability and need. Sometimes willingness to feel our need is accompanied by an unexpected flood of tears. I remember times in my life when tears flowed, catching me by surprise. The dam broke when I didn't even know anything had been stored up behind my wall of determination to "bear up," "buck up," and "hold up" during a time of great stress. What a relief it was when the hole in the dike came unplugged, and released floodwaters I had been holding back. We need to get beyond the cultural influences that have caused us to think we have to be strong, independent, solve our own problems, and be tough.

I encourage you to be willing to receive comfort. We cannot create a hug by ourselves! A hug is a two-person event. I cannot feel hugged just by trying to feel hugged. In the same way, God's comfort, God's gift of hope, comes from His direct action upon your spirit. You cannot create the feeling of His comfort or His hope simply by imagining it. It is a specific gift of His Holy Spirit to you, as you surrender your will to it. Ask Him for it. He will not refuse you. Be willing to receive it to replace your feelings of hopelessness and helplessness.

Caution: The saying, "God helps those who help themselves" does not come from the Bible. Somebody said it because it sounds good. But it's not Biblical. God's Word tells us clearly that God is the helper of the helpless! Big difference! You do not have to help God give you His comfort, His peace, His joy, His reassurance, or His hope. He gives it to you simply because you are willing, honest, vulnerable, and ask Him for your need. "Come boldly before the throne of God to find help in your time of need." (Hebrews 4:16)

The fruit of the Spirit is love, joy, peace, goodness, faith, gentleness, meekness, long-suffering, and self-control. It is fruit of the Spirit, not the fruit of our efforts. Not the fruit of our imaginations. God knows we cannot produce these qualities by self-will and self-effort. He does it all for us, often in spite of ourselves, but always when we ask it of Him. He gives freely as we submit our will, surrender, admit our inadequacies and weaknesses, and rest in His provision. He will give it, for it is His will that we have these great blessings in our lives: freedom from fear, anxiety, false guilt, depression, discouragement, hopelessness, and every other negative emotion that plagues the human condition. There are innumerable examples of these throughout God's Word to prove His interest and involvement to give victory over such things to His people.

Christ has won the victory for us, and the fruit of the Spirit is constantly being formed in us by His work on our behalf. We only need to give up our willingness to tolerate and live with those all-too-familiar negative emotions. Sometimes it takes a while before we become completely exhausted and fed up with the bad feelings; so much that we can't wait to be rid of them! The patient love of God is there when we finally make it to that point of surrender. His perfect faithfulness meets us where we are. I can almost hear Him saying with a smile, "Okay, Honey, now that you're ready, I'm here to give you peace of mind and hope for the future that will bless your socks off."

Although God hears every prayer and answers our immediate needs, a complete transformation of all our negative thoughts doesn't happen all at once. Oh, how I wish it would! No, it's a walk of faith God desires us to live out, day by day, year by year, piece by piece, in the same way that we walk step by step in the physical world to reach our destination. Not an instantaneous "Beam me up, Scotty!" As we experience God's power each time we call out to Him, we gain alertness and wisdom for future mental and emotional battles when they come. We are better prepared for them, because we see them lurking in the shadows, and we can call them out for what they are. That's how the enemy is defeated—when he is exposed and fought with the spiritual weapons of our warfare. But as we have learned, the enemy has to be detected and located first! This is a spiritual attribute you are developing as you take each step of faith.

Each time we get victory in a battle, our spiritual ranks are strengthened, and our battle strategies are honed. We begin to detect the enemy early in the attack, and we remember the triumph of earlier struggles. We then can begin rejoicing as a victorious overcomer in that arena. This is repeated throughout our lives, and each time we gain ground over the enemy, it is with greater joy and freedom. Through multiple events, prayer, and surrender, we discover shining facets of our salvation that have increasing sparkle and brilliance.

15   Perfect Love

"Perfect love casts out fear…"   I John 4:18

Perfect love. It may, at first, seem as if it is off-topic, but it is just the opposite. It is a suitable wrap-up to solidify our thinking. It is from I John 4:18: "There is no fear in love; but perfect love casts out fear, because fear involves torment …"

I have puzzled over this verse many times for many years. "What does love have to do with fear?" I asked myself each time I read it, without getting an answer. They do not seem to be opposites. "How can love work to cast out fear?" Without answers, I shelved my questions, shrugging a bit, and figured one day it would come to light.

God is faithful to patiently teach us, and doesn't seem to mind our puzzling over His Word.

Today I realize why I was perplexed. I was missing the key thought. Its omission in my thinking skewed the whole verse for me. The key word is "perfect." Perfect love. Not my love, which is imperfect even at its best. Nor is it a love that I can work on to perfect it to such a dazzling point that it will naturally cast out fear. No. That would be exhausting futility. The only perfect love is the love of God. It is His perfect love that casts out fear, not my own. His love indwells the hearts of believers by the power and presence of His Holy Spirit; it is not anything I conjure up with effort. It is His gift, living in me in all its power and provision. His love for me is perfect, complete, entire, lacking nothing. His love is powerful, protecting, and purposeful. His love is encompassing, always present with me, always full, never running on fumes.

God is love. It is His love that casts out fear. How? When I am aware of the power and omnipresence of His love, that is what assures me, secures me, and casts out fears that torment. "God is for me. What can man do unto me?" With the Lord of the universe for me, what possible circumstance or threatening force is any match for what His love has planned and provided for me? The protection is more than just knowing about this love. It is dwelling in it, absorbing the truth of His constant Loving Presence within me through the Holy Spirit. That great, perfect Love is in me, always. It is the sustaining part of my life.

Perhaps I don't take enough time to focus on God's love for me. It can become too familiar a thought glibly quoted, kind of like "Jesus Loves Me, This I Know," so that I hear the words too quickly, and don't really, really focus on them. Jesus spent His life on earth proving His love to us through His healings, teachings, sufferings, sacrificial death, and amazing resurrection appearances. He ascended into heaven and rules from there in all power and glory. His love is unconditional and extravagant—matchless.

This is truth, but at times it is a real challenge to hold onto it because I never see things with the clarity that God sees them. Bad things happen to good people, just as good things happen to bad people. It's an enigma in our limited vision of the big picture. However, God's vision is completely unhindered. His plans are at times mysterious and often invisible to us. But He oversees all our ways, knows every circumstance, "our down-sitting and our up-rising," and His perfect plan arches over every happening in the lives of His children. He manages it all for ultimate good.

I am sure you have detected a theme throughout the chapters of this book. Hopefully, you noticed there is overlapping and interweaving as we have applied truth to different examples. That is because most of our negative emotions arise from a single dominant force—fear. Fear of the unknown, fear of losing someone or something dear to us, fear of not being valued, fear of being insignificant, fear of the future, fear of not being good enough, you name it. Fear is a despicable dictator of negative emotions.

But, as we have seen, in our corner we have the victorious Champion of Love who defeats the dictates of the world, the flesh, and the devil. All of God's Word is a harmonic symphony of truth for our real life needs. The answers to all our negative emotions are encapsulated in I John 4. There we read the surprising prescription for all our fears—discover and dwell in the perfect love of God. That has been the victorious interwoven piece of the pattern in every chapter's theme.

"Draw near to God and He will draw near to you. Resist the devil (and evil, fearsome things) and he (the devil and accompanying fears) will flee from you." (James 4:8)

It is good news that the answer always comes back to the central issue of God's perfect love. We don't have to keep track of what to do about this or that negative feeling. It is clear and foundational. His perfect love is the fabric of our umbrella. The spokes of the umbrella are the wonderful specific scriptures God has given us to apply to our particular situation. The wonderful reality of our place under God's umbrella is that the provision and protection of God is complete and always perfect!

It doesn't matter how menacing the challenge looks and feels to us. God is our refuge and our strength.

"Be strong, therefore, in the Lord, and in the power of His might...above all, taking up the shield of faith by which you will be able to quench all the fiery darts of the wicked one." (Ephesians 6:16)

His Word, along with our believing (if only with a mustard-seed-size faith) that God is faithful and cannot lie, is the beginning of victory. Our willingness to cast aside doubtful and worrisome thoughts in favor of what He promises invites God's breath to blow out the fearsome fires. And this He does, because He is Love in perfection, and Love never fails to provide for its loved ones. The gentle breath He breathed upon us when He gave us life is also the powerful blast that He blows upon His enemies like a whirlwind.

No, He never fails. We are the ones who fail. We fail to remember we are children of the King. We fail to remember that He is always on our side. We fail to remind ourselves of all He provides. We fail to read His promises. Sometimes we even fail to ask.

God asks very little of us, only that we believe. Jesus said, "Oh, ye of little faith," and that's what I am at times, "Oh, me of little faith." But it's not what I want to be. And that's exactly what I tell my Lord, "My faith isn't what it ought to be. And it's not nearly what you are worthy of. Forgive me. Increase my faith. Give me help to hang in here and believe you are doing important things in my life. Help me to trust you that it is for good. Help me to be patient with the process, and to trust in my heart what my head knows you are—loving, wise, good, and faithful."

In this modern day, the church has not always kept us mindful of profound truths regarding the testing of our faith, persecutions, spiritual warfare, and the mighty efforts of Satan, our enemy who suggests and influences our thoughts, instigating fears and lighting roaring fires in our emotions. Few speakers want to talk about these issues to a crowd who came to hear happy thoughts and good news. But good news is always firmly attached to biblical examples of trials and distresses. The good news is that God is present and we are promised victory.

It's important to keep in mind that we are continually in spiritual battles against spirits of wickedness that are invisible—evil forces whose goal is to shake our foundations, weaken our faith, and destroy our sense of God's love and faithfulness. It is imperative to remember the Bible tells us to put on the armor of God to withstand the onslaught. We are to stand and hold our position in confidence. "Therefore take up the whole armor of God, that you may be able to withstand in the evil day, and having done all, to stand." (Ephesians 6:13)

We are not meant to fight these battles by sheer willpower and determined mindset. Rather, we are meant to apply our will and desire in prayer, and to rely on God for His strength, illumination, and protection, to persevere through the hardships and sufferings that are common to all—both believers and unbelievers.

We all suffer similar woes, but we believers have the incredible privilege of being sheltered under God's Umbrella of Love during the storms. It is for His glory, and for eternal rewards which will make these sufferings pale in comparison after this brief life on earth. "Consider that the sufferings of this time are not worthy to be compared with the glory that will be revealed in us." (Romans 8:18) No wonder the Lord God takes our side in the battle and fights for us. It will be eternal glory to display His victories forever, honoring His awesome, perfect love for His beloved children.

We can endure because we have the confidence and comforting knowledge that although we experience suffering as do others in the world, we, as children of God in Christ Jesus, have a sure foundation, a solid rock for our footing, and a loving Hand to hold fast while we walk by faith. God's enemy, the father of lies and fear, cannot overcome the power of God. Perfect love casts out fear.

ABIDE

To be made perfect in love relies on faith to receive it and dwell in it. We must discipline our thoughts so that fear is cast out. Don't allow yourself to give time to think about the fearful thing. Give time to think about God's greatness, goodness, love, and faithfulness. He does what He says He will do. He casts out fear with His perfect love in order to bless us and help us overcome negative emotions because He knows every fear has torment. What parent is willing to have his child feel torment? None. That's why we can trust and know that God, who is Love, will cast out fear and the torment that drives it. So I ask Him.

James, the disciple, grew up with his half-brother Jesus and surely saw amazing things come from Jesus' divine power and heart. He informs us that we can miss receiving all that God wants to give us and work in us. We can lose out simply by neglecting to bring our request to God. Pride gets in the way. It is a mistake to think, oh, I can handle this one. I don't need to ask for God's help. James wrote, "You have not because you ask not." So I ask! I must not ever think that maybe I'm just destined to have fear and torment, and so I will resign myself to it. That is not God's will for us. That is surrendering to an enemy spirit of fear when we have God-powered weapons for conquering it.

He who fears has not been made perfect in Love. If I'm fear-filled, it's not because God is withholding His perfect love and grace. He has a boundless supply to bestow, to restore my peace of mind and eliminate my fear. As David wrote, "I sought the Lord, and He heard me and delivered me from all my fears." God has provided His perfect Love for me to dwell in. The door is always open to that shelter of Love and peace. If I am fear-filled, it's because of my failure to drink in, meditate, and believe that His perfect Love is within me and surrounding me, protecting me from that which I fear.

CHOOSE
Our job is to choose which dominion we want to live in. This is what "work out your own salvation" means. Believe and receive! When I choose to walk in the realm of faith, believe God's promises, and allow Him to work it out in me, I have chosen freedom from fear and torment. What a deal! God has an unending supply of everything I need for life and godliness. And so, I take a deep breath and stretch out my trembling faith to eagerly receive the promises and provisions God offers me—free for the faith-taking, wrapped up in His Love. His provision is just what I need. Events and other people may disappoint me, but God does not. He upholds me in His loving hand.

"Fear not, for I am with you; Be not dismayed, for I am your God. I will strengthen you, Yes, I will help you, I

226

will uphold you with My righteous right hand." (Isaiah 41:10)

TRUST

The second half of 1 John 4:18 about perfect love goes like this: "...But he who fears has not been made perfect in love." This gave me pause, because at first I thought it meant my nagging fear was proof of my incapacity to love well. That's not it at all. Remember? It's not about my love; it's about the magnanimous love of God. It is about His perfect love, freely given to me through His Son Jesus and manifested and lived out by the Spirit. The verse is pointing out my only role is something very different. It is simply to trust God's unfailing Love. If I am suffering or wallowing in fear, it is because I am not walking in faith. I am not staying alert to the boundless love of God that wraps around me like a warm blanket and empowers me from within. It is a "Hey you!" kind of statement like, "Oh, so you're afraid? Heads up! Are you forgetting that my perfect Love is here for you? I will be with you. I will strengthen you. I am here to help and uphold you. You don't need to be afraid. Refocus! Refocus! I am about to show you that I'm going to take care of all this because I love you! Trust my love."

We may not always see the results as something we would characterize as "love." Love sometimes takes a different tack than what we expect or prefer, just as a child may not see rules or consequences as being favorable or loving. But they are in place for the good of the child and safety. We have already settled in our minds that God is a God of love. More than that—God *is* Love. (1 John 4:8) His ways are perfect, regardless of how they look or feel at a moment in time. It will play out right.

Accepting an unexpected result as coming through the Love filter that God holds is a life-changing aspect of walking by faith. No one has claimed this kind of faith is easy. Unexpected results are not always the kind we prefer. But believers through the centuries and at the present time testify that tenacious faith's reward produces peace and joy for life. When we have experienced it, the treasure of its powerful effects is undeniable and worth more than gold. It becomes the chosen direction for our thinking and emotions for the next challenge. Believe and trust.

ACT

When these three attitudes are employed—Abide, Choose, Trust—new, powerful brain circuitry begins to be formed, and calmer emotions develop bit by bit. Each experience strengthens our faith. We see and feel the changes, and so do others who are looking on. We find we have control we didn't know was possible. We receive freedom from overwhelming negative emotions as we ACT—Abide, Choose, and Trust.

It is not our self-effort. It is perfect love, casting out fear. And really, as we are seeing, it is not complicated. Jesus invites us to come to Him like a little child. "Cast all your care upon Him, for He cares for you." (1 Peter 5:7)

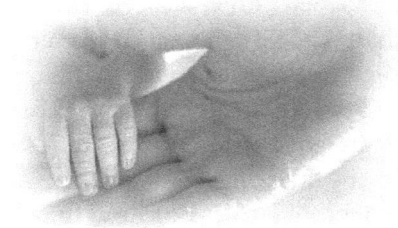

"This is the victory that overcomes the world, even our faith." 1 John 5:4

"Let the word of Christ dwell in you richly." Colossians 3:16

Your victories will be won in proportion to the time and attention you give them, using the powerful and unfailing weapons that God has given us—His Word, His authority, faith, and choice. I pray that you will dive deeply into His Love and Truth, and experience beautiful freedom to enjoy each day, day by day, without unnecessary burdens of emotions you were never meant to carry. Celebrate each victory, no matter how small. They all add up to build new habits of thinking and responding. The triumphant Christ holds your hand to guide you into your abundant life.

"For the Lord God is a sun and shield; he bestows favor and honor. No good thing does the Lord withhold from those who walk uprightly." Psalm 84:11

NOTES:

What were your "aha" moments? Write them here to help you remember what God is impressing upon you:

NOTES:
Write your "aha" Scriptures here to keep them handy for when you need them:

OTHER BOOKS by Marilee Donivan

Faith Refined—*Holding on When Life is Falling Apart*
Springs of Hope—*Meditations of the Heart*
Beginning Watercolor Painting
Wings for Kevin
Kandu and the Magic Meadow
The Parable of Kandu—*A Story within a Story*

More information can be found at
www.amazon.com
or
www.sunrisemountainbooks.com

ABOUT THE AUTHOR

Marilee Donivan is certified in Caring for People God's Way through the Center for Biblical Counseling, and is a member of the American Association of Christian Counselors. She was a classroom teacher and a student teacher supervisor. Her greatest desire in life is to serve God by encouraging others. She shares God's victorious principles from her own hard-fought battles and joy-filled experiences. She enjoys watercolor painting and has illustrated several of her books with her artwork.

Marilee welcomes your correspondence and will answer it personally. She can be contacted at this email address:

mdonivan@sunrisemountainbooks.com

FAITH
Refined-
HOLDING ON WHEN LIFE IS FALLING APART

WITH CONVERSATION STARTERS
MARILEE DONIVAN

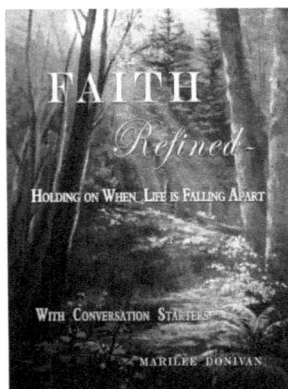

Now with
Conversation Starters
for Book Clubs and Bible Studies

FAITH *Refined* —**Holding on
When Life is Falling Apart:**
With Conversation Starters

In the midst of confusion and uncertainty, you desperately want something to hang onto for stability and hope. What do you do when unwelcome changes suddenly reshape your life?

The author's experiences of losses and miracles, disillusionment and hope, depression and joy ring with authenticity. So does her faith, which weathered attacks from spiritual forces and her own ragged emotions in this riveting true story.

Her powerful real-life examples will fortify your faith and inspire you to press on and experience God's amazing love in new ways.

Readers asked for discussion questions to use in Book Clubs and Bible studies. This new edition answers the call. The compelling narrative is a worthwhile journey through trials, questions, and victories with updates since the first printing. Conversation Starters at the end of each chapter invite reflection and meaningful conversation about experiences and beliefs. Use them to nourish personal spiritual growth and mutual support in a group setting.

198 pages.
ISBN 978-1-940728-12-4

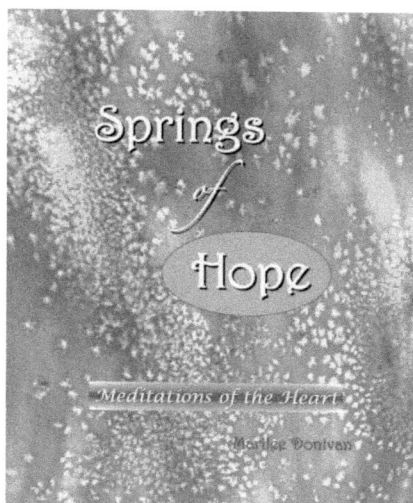

Springs of Hope is a collection of 20 full-color, full-size watercolor paintings and devotional thoughts to provide moments of peaceful reflections for hope and encouragement. Created for bedside reading or coffee table browsing, it brings color and abstract designs along with some impressionistic scenes to explore. As a pick-me-up gift, it is like a series of colorful greeting cards, reminding someone God is thinking about them every day. **8″ x 10″** size.

46 pages.
ISBN 978-0-9842362-7-5

www.ingramcontent.com/pod-product-compliance
Lightning Source LLC
LaVergne TN
LVHW051625080426
835511LV00016B/2180